KINGS AND PRIESTS TO OUR GOD

Keys to effective prayer

Cover design – Clive Thompson

Author's Photograph – Stephen Michael

To contact the author: email - pilbrough@mweb.co.za

CONTENTS

ACKNOWLEDGEMENTS

Firstly, my thanks go to my wife, Helena, for the many hours she spent diligently knocking my manuscript into shape, and to Bernadette Varner, for the final touches.

My thanks go to the many Christian leaders who have shaped and encouraged my spiritual growth over the years. Their influence has been invaluable, and the Lord will reward them accordingly.

ACKNOWLEDGEMENT

FOREWORD

Little did I know when I invited Steve to teach on the topic of prayer in the Bible school I was leading, that 30-some years later, I would be asked to write the Foreword to his book on the very topic he taught so well.

I have known Steve for well over 30 years. The biggest credit to his character would be that he was one of a few people who stood with me at the lowest point of my life. This is the friend I had in my corner, praying kingly and priestly prayers over my life. Thank you, Steve, for your prayers in those dark days. I am forever grateful, and honestly believe that I am where I am today because of the grace of God and you praying out of the revelation God had given you.

Years ago, my pastor, Chris Hodges, gave me one simple and profound revelation on the topic of prayer. He said, "As a leader, you cannot delegate prayer". It may be obvious, and yet many believers would say that their biggest internal difficulty is how to maintain the consistency of their personal prayer life. I do not think their struggle is over *believing* in prayer, but that they do not know *how* to pray. Even Jesus' disciples asked Him - *Teach us how to pray.*

My amazing wife would quickly testify to the fact that I am not Mr Handyman around the house. You may be surprised when I tell you that we do have a toolbox at home. But I very seldom open it. When I do, I will inevitably look for my go-to tool. It is one of those tools that looks like a Swiss army knife on steroids. Why do I like it? Because it is a tool that I can use in most situations that require my handyman's attention.

We all have a toolbox for our prayer life. Many of us have only used the multi-tool prayer that does not always fit the job. Steve outlines amazingly in this book how many excellent prayers we have at our disposal. Using the right prayer tool gives us confidence that our prayer will be scriptural, and therefore effective. Maybe we use the key of David when we need to open or close situations, or the prayer of agreement, or maybe it is the prayer of faith. What tools are in your prayer box?

In this book 'Kings and Priests to our God', Steve will introduce you to a prayer box with two compartments. In one compartment are the prayers that we use as a king. In the other, are prayers we pray as a priest. It will be a game-changer for your prayer life.

It is no surprise to me that this revelation Steve received over 30 years ago is being released into the body of Christ at such a time as this. May this revelation spread throughout the world and empower a new generation of spiritual kings and priests, who will unashamedly take charge in the unseen realm of prayer and become the waymakers for the plan of God in these end-time days, ushering in an open heaven for a harvest of souls, the Church has not seen before.

Dr Desmond Frey

Lead Pastor, Internationals at Buchegg Church Zürich, Switzerland.

Board Director, HarvestNet International, Ephrata, Pennsylvania, USA.

INTRODUCTION

As I sat studying in my outside rondavel bedroom at my parents' house in Harare, Zimbabwe in 1985, and preparing for the Bible school classes on prayer that I was soon to teach, I was asking the Lord, "How can I teach the correct way to pray and make it real and practical for my students?". I had only been born again for three years and I was grappling with my understanding of the spirit world. Being scientifically inclined, the thought of speaking to a being that I could not see, took quite a lot of mental adjustment. The walls of the box that was my life were blown apart when I accepted Christ as my Lord and Saviour, and before me was this glorious new unseen world to explore. In my previous 22 years, I had only known the world that my five senses could detect, and here I was faced with a whole new unseen world, with the Creator of the universe, at its centre. I needed this study into prayer to catch up on the development of my sixth sense. I needed to learn, but more importantly, I needed to pray. E M Bounds said, "No learning can make up for the failure to pray. No earnestness, no diligence, no study, no gifts will supply its lack".

Having been asked to teach a Bible school class on prayer right after graduating from a one-year part time Bible school course, in hindsight, was absolutely crazy. I do not know who was crazier - the dean of the Bible school for asking me, or me for accepting. But I am forever grateful for that opportunity which also helped me discover that I was able to teach, and I loved the journey. Studying for this class propelled me to dig deep into the Bible and to extract truth concerning communication with God. It is strangely natural, but in your spirit, you know how right the exercise of prayer is, especially when you start to hear His voice in reply.

Most of us know about Jesus' instructions on prayer in Matt 6:5-7, where we are not to pray to be seen but to go into our room and pray to our heavenly Father. Then Jesus adds - *And when you pray, do not use vain repetitions as the heathens do. For they think that they will be heard for their many words. Therefore, do not be like them. For your Father knows the things you have need of before you ask Him.* He then goes on to tell the disciples how to pray in what we now call the Lord's Prayer, and rather than this scripture answering my many questions, I was faced with many more. For example, I needed to know exactly what words we should use when we pray in secret to avoid repetition. Another conundrum was that in the Lord's Prayer we pray - *forgive us our debts as we forgive our debtors.* I knew that we had already been forgiven of our sins at the cross, so what was Jesus telling us to do here? I needed answers before I could properly teach prayer, so I dived even deeper into the Word. God opened the eyes of my understanding so that I had enough answers to my questions. I began seeing results in my prayer life and was able to better instruct my students.

There are amazing promises in the New Testament, for example – *whatever you ask in My name, that I will do, that the Father may be glorified in the Son. If you ask anything in My name, I will do it* (John 14:13-14). Wow! What a promise, so powerful, with only one condition - *ask in My name.* Just over the page in John 15:7, there is another promise - *If you abide in Me, and My words abide in you, you will ask what you desire, and it shall be done for you.* What an awesome promise that He will answer my prayer, the only condition being to abide in Him and He in me.

I wrestled with understanding these scriptures and the Lord led me to dig into the Greek meaning of the words in the scriptures I was studying. My training on how to study was sketchy at best, having attended only one year of part time Bible school the previous year, and even so, hermeneutics and exegesis were foreign words to me. All I had was my tome of a Strongs Concordance, a Vine's Expository Dictionary of New Testament Words, my King James Bible and the Holy Spirit. *But the anointing which you have received from Him abides in you, and you do not need that anyone teach you* (1 John 2:27). I had no access to commentaries or teachings of great men of God, and this worked for me as I had to dig out the truths for myself, with only the guidance of the Holy Spirit. Since then, I have read excellent teachings on prayer, the likes of Andrew Murray, Brother Lawrence, Andrew Wommack, E M Bounds and John Alcock. Each has a different perspective and emphasis and similarly, I hope that you will find in this book on praying as kings and priests, a fresh perspective on this very important discipline of our Christian lives.

There are many kinds of prayer mentioned in the epistles, as in 1 Tim 2:1 *Therefore I exhort first of all that supplications, prayers, intercessions, and giving of thanks be made for all men.* Much has been written on these types of prayer which is very helpful for our understanding on how to pray effectively. But as you will discover in this book, these prayers are all priestly types of prayer. The kingly type of prayer is absent from this scripture in Timothy, but we find it hidden in scriptures like Mark 11:23-24. Speaking to the mountain is definitely a type of prayer that we can easily miss and verse 24 confirms this - *Therefore I say to you, whatever things you ask when you pray, believe that you receive them, and you will have them.* This is kingly prayer and we need a clear understanding on how it differs from priestly prayer in order to pray effectively in the authority we have in Christ.

Therefore I also … do not cease to give thanks for you, making mention of you in my prayers … the eyes of your understanding being enlightened; that you may know what is … the exceeding greatness of His power towards us who believe, according to the working of His mighty power which He worked in Christ when He raised Him from the dead and seated Him at His right hand in the heavenly places (Eph 1:15-20). That same breathtaking power that raised Jesus from the dead is in us and is available for us to use as we pray for His kingdom to be established on earth as it is in heaven.

This book is a distillation of what I have learned about prayer over the last 40 years. No work on prayer can ever be complete and my journey is far from over, but I trust that you will find truths in this book which will enable you to become more effective in prayer so that you can see positive changes in yourself, your family, church, community, and even in your nation. We all desire to see the promises of God manifest around us - *Ask and you will receive, that your joy may be full* (John 16:24b). The study of prayer is a vital work, especially as the world system that we live in gets crazier and darker by the day. The time you spend reading this book will be time well spent, as long as you pray and not just mentally assent to the principles expounded herein.

According to E M Bounds, "No man can do a great and enduring work for God who is not a man of prayer, and no man can be a man of prayer who does not give much time to praying".

KINGS AND PRIESTS

For You were slain and have redeemed us to God by Your blood out of every tribe and tongue and people and nation, and have made us kings and priests to our God; and we shall reign on the earth (Rev 5:9b-10).

Back in 1985, as I read this scripture and tried to understand how it related to prayer, I realised that we instinctively understand the role of a priest in the Bible because most of us have experienced how a modern-day priest serves in churches today. He leads the congregation in prayer to God by using words to connect with the unseen world. This led me to so many more questions: How does the priest know how to pray? What words does he use? How does God answer?

I realised that the only connection we have with the unseen supernatural world is our words. In the beginning, God swung the universe into existence using only His words. He used words to commune with Adam and Eve in the garden. Words instructed Noah to build the ark, told Abram to leave his home and Lot to leave Sodom. An angel brought the Word of God to Mary about Jesus' birth, and at Pentecost, the Holy Spirit gave words of many tongues to the disciples, declaring the wonder of a glorious God.

Words are our bridge to the supernatural. God's words changed the actions of men. God's words in the mouth of the Old Testament prophets changed the course of history for individuals and nations. Jesus' words brought a new dispensation to the earth as to the understanding of our loving heavenly Father. Jesus, by His words, healed the sick, cleansed lepers and delivered many from demons.

So, words are the key, but as I looked at all the examples in the Bible where words changed situations, they were different words and there were different ways of saying these words. How are we to know which words to say, how to say them and when to use them? The more I studied, it dawned on me that sometimes the words were spoken to men on behalf of God, and on other occasions they were said to God on behalf of men. Sometimes the speaker was pleading with God for a person in a request, and on other occasions the speaker was declaring the words of God to people for them to change. The pleading to God prayer was like a priest in a position of humility making a request. The prayer declaring God's Word was like a king making a decree to effect change in his kingdom.

*To Him who loved us and washed us from our sins in His own blood, and has made us **kings and priests** to His God and Father, to Him be glory and dominion forever and ever (*Rev 1:5b-6).

It started to make sense when I realised that God has called us to be both kings and priests for Him on the earth. This phrase is repeated as follows -

*And have made us **kings and priests** to our God; and we shall reign on the earth (Rev 5:10).*

If we accepted Jesus' sacrifice and have been born again, we are elevated to be kings and priests to the Father. We are the agents of change on the earth, kingly ambassadors of the King declaring the will of the King on the earth and reconciling His subjects to Him. We preach God's Word to all who will listen, showing them the way, the truth and the life, as ambassadors. But firstly, it is necessary to prepare the ground in prayer - claiming the ground from demonic possession and sickness in kingly prayer, and preparing hearts to receive the incorruptible Word of God in priestly prayer. Both types of prayer are very different, spoken differently and to different recipients.

It has always been God's desire to speak and relate to us face to face. In the garden of Eden, God spoke with Adam and Eve face to face in the 'cool of the evening'. Sin spoilt that and created a barrier between God and man, but God still desired His people to relate to Him directly.

Sin had created an impenetrable barrier between God and His people, so He implemented a way to closely relate to His 'set apart ones'. Through Moses, the Law and the blood sacrifices, God made a way to meet with the Israelites as close as He could without destroying them.

Now therefore, if you will indeed obey My voice and keep My covenant, then you shall be a special treasure to Me above all people; for the earth is Mine. And you shall be to Me a kingdom of priests and a holy nation (Ex 19:5-6a).

Notice the language of this scripture is a little different to Rev 5:10. At the base of Mt Sinai, because of sin, the Israelites could only approach God as priests. In fact, it was His desire that the whole nation of Israel would be His priests. In Ex 19:8 and again in Ex 24:3, the Israelites said, *"All that the Lord has spoken we will do."* The sight of God descending onto Mt Sinai was so frightening that the Israelites wanted Moses to do the speaking for them. And he did. Moses went into the Tabernacle regularly when the cloud of God's presence descended, and *the Lord spoke to Moses face to face, as a man speaks to his friend (Ex 33:11).*

Jesus came to earth and made the perfect sacrifice on the cross, and *having wiped out the handwriting of requirements that was against us ... having nailed it to the cross (Col 2:14),* He made it possible for us to commune with God again, symbolised by the temple curtain being torn, top to bottom. Sin was forever dealt with, and this restored man to the position that Adam and Eve had with God. Under the Law, man could relate to God as a priest, and only a certain tribe of a certain nation could do that. When Jesus won back man's authority on the earth, we could once again approach God freely as priests and represent God again on the earth as kings.

All authority has been given to Me in heaven and on earth. Go therefore ... (Matt 28:18b-19a).

We, as disciples of Jesus Christ, have been mandated to rule and reign and bring the kingdom of heaven to earth. It was impossible, before Jesus died as the perfect sacrifice, for us to have authority over the devil and his cohorts. Now it is our right and obligation to take authority over the works of the devil and declare the Acceptable Year of the Lord. Jubilee is here and all captives have been made free through His blood.

Back to prayer. We can now pray as kings and priests: as kings we take dominion over the work of the enemy, healing the sick, opening blind eyes and delivering the oppressed; as priests we forgive people their sins (John 20:23), speak the blessings of our covenant over people and pray for blind spiritual eyes to be opened so that people can accept Christ and be born again. As kings we pray in authority; as priests we pray in supplication.

ASK

In the last chapter, we saw that there are two very different ways to pray as kings and priests. When we pray as kings, it is with authority and commanding things to change. As priests, we are requesting for the Holy Spirit to positively influence people's lives.

All those years ago, while studying for my Bible school class, the Holy Spirit taught me the scriptural basis for these two main types of prayer in the simple little word 'ask'. When we pray, we are usually asking. I discovered that there was a vast difference in the meanings of 'ask' in the Greek, the language in which the New Testament was written. In English, we only have one word for 'ask'. In the Greek, there are two very different words translated as 'ask'.

In John 16:23-24 we see the two different words for 'ask' used.

*And in that day you will **ask** Me nothing. Most assuredly, I say to you, whatever you **ask** the Father in My name He will give you. Until now you have **asked** nothing in My name. **Ask** and you will receive, that your joy may be full.*

What a superb promise that seems to have no conditions to it - ask and you will receive. Actually, there are conditions, and they are hidden in the meanings of the word 'ask'. This scripture actually does not make much sense unless we know the meaning of the 'ask' used.

Also, we need to understand which 'day' is being referred to and the time referred to by Jesus in saying 'until now'. Big changes happened at the cross, and in this scripture, Jesus is referring to two different times - before the cross and His sacrifice, and after. As we will see, this makes a huge difference to how we 'ask'. Before the cross, Jesus had not established the New Covenant, and access to the Father was prevented as we were still in our sins. After the cross, we are redeemed by His blood, and symbolically in the tearing of the temple veil, believers now have free access to the Holy of Holies and the presence of the Father. Let us read John 16:23-24 again, replacing the word 'ask' with the original Greek word used.

*And in that day you will **erotao** Me nothing. Most assuredly, I say to you, whatever you **aiteo** the Father in My name He will give you. Until now you have **aiteo** nothing in My name. **Aiteo** and you will receive, that your joy may be full.*

The Revised English Version Commentary (www.revised-englishversion.com) explains the different use of the word 'ask' in this passage very well:

Aiteo means to ask, but very forcefully … ask for with claim on receipt of an answer, demand. In contrast, erotao means to put a query to someone; ask a question, seeking information.

A simple explanation of the two words is as follows:

Aiteo - to ask based on our covenant rights; to demand something due.

Erotao - to ask as a favour.

I have had some people object to these definitions as they say "you cannot demand of God. After all He is God, and you cannot make Him do anything". That is true, but we are not demanding God to do something, but rather we are calling on the provision already made for us at the cross. Jesus said in Matt 26:28 *For this is My blood of the new covenant which is shed for many* ... The New Covenant has promises which are ours to appropriate. We claim these promises and do not beg for them. It is the same as a child going to his mother and saying, "I am hungry. I want to eat". He knows instinctively that if he is hungry, it is his right to ask (demand) and it is his mother's obligation to provide food. The child does not beg or negotiate with his mother to persuade her to feed him. There could be negotiation on the timing of the meal or what sort of food it will be, but the fact is that the child has a posture of demanding food not begging. The situation would be very different if the child was at his friend's house. He could not demand of his friend's mother for food. She has no obligation to feed her son's friend. She could feed him based on his **erotao**, whereas in his own house he will **aiteo** for food.

The passage in John 16:23-24 makes much more sense when we expand the words 'ask' using the Greek meanings. Furthermore, it is very important to understand what 'in that day' means in this passage. Jesus is referring to the day when He was to establish the New Covenant in His blood:

And in that day, after the cross, you will beg me nothing as a favour. Most assuredly, I say to you, whatever you demand according to the New Covenant, the Father in My name, He will give you. Until now, before the cross, you have demanded nothing of the New Covenant in My name as I have not yet died to establish your rights in it. When it is done, demand of your New Covenant and you will receive everything that has been paid for in the New Covenant, that your joy may be full (my paraphrase).

It is important to know what this New Covenant has 'bought' for us and it is up to us to appropriate. You will notice that this passage says 'in My name'. Children who have the family surname are endowed with certain rights as sons and daughters, and likewise, we who believe and are called Christians, sons of God, co-heirs with Christ, have rights by carrying our family name.

We see the promises of the New Covenant in many scriptures that describe Jesus' mission on earth.

Luke 4:18-19 *The Spirit of the Lord is upon Me, because He has anointed Me to preach the **gospel to the poor;** He has sent Me to **heal the brokenhearted,** to proclaim **liberty to the captives** and recovery of **sight to the blind,** to **set at liberty those who are oppressed;** to proclaim the **acceptable year of the Lord.***

1 Peter 2:24 *who Himself bore our **sins** in His own body on the tree, that we, having died to sins, might live for righteousness - by whose stripes you were **healed**.*

2 Cor 8:9 *For you know the grace of our Lord Jesus Christ, that though He was rich, yet for your sakes He became poor, that you through **His poverty might become rich**.*

The purpose of this book is not to debate whether healing and prosperity are in the atonement. I want to simply present what the scriptures say about the New Covenant so we can have access to the promises through belief in His sacrifice on the cross. You cannot **aiteo** something that has not been paid for with His blood.

Many promises in the Old Testament were looking forward to the perfect fulfilment in Jesus at the cross, and so we can claim them as ours through **aiteo.**

Exodus 15:26b *For I am the Lord who **heals** you.*

Exodus 22:25-26 *So you shall serve the Lord your God, and He will **bless your bread and your water**. And I will take **sickness** away from the midst of you. No one shall suffer **miscarriage** or be **barren** in your land; I will fulfil the **number of your days**.*

Isaiah 53:4-5 *Surely He has borne our **griefs** and carried our **sorrows**; Yet we esteemed Him stricken, smitten by God, and afflicted. But He was wounded for our **transgressions**, He was bruised for our **iniquities**; the chastisement for our **peace** was upon Him, and by His stripes we are **healed**.*

From these scriptures we can **aiteo** the following:

- We are free from lack, spiritually and materially.
- We have healing from a broken heart when we are rejected and suffer loss of any kind as we have direct access to a loving heavenly Father.
- We are set free from the chains of addiction, abuse and iniquity as we are accepted as His child despite our circumstances.
- Our sight has been restored spiritually and physically as the power of sin that blinded us has been destroyed at the cross.
- We are set free of any kind of oppression as He cares for us and lifts the burden of sin from us.
- We are healed in our bodies because of the merciless beating that He took in His sinless body, and we are healed in our souls by Him taking wicked mocking, jealousy, envy and every kind of mental abuse to the cross where it died with Him.
- Our food and water are blessed as we receive it with thanksgiving.
- We are set free from miscarriage and infertility in our families.
- We will live blessed all our days until we are satisfied.
- Our sins and transgressions are paid for past, present and future. They have no hold on us anymore.
- We have peace as we are now one with our loving heavenly Father, and He will never be angry with

us again. We are in Him and He is in us, and nothing can separate us from His love.

- He has declared Jubilee over us - making everything new again, despite our past. (The Acceptable Year of the Lord is the year of Jubilee in the Jewish Law; the 50th year when all slaves are set free, and all property bonded for debt is returned to the original owners. Jubilee says it all.) We are free from all the oppression of the devil.

These are the things we can **aiteo** in His name. Whatever you **aiteo**, invoking the name of the One who did it for you at the cross, you will have, and you will be overjoyed as a result. The understanding in this passage is that you have to believe that He did it for you. Otherwise, you will not **aiteo** Him for them, like the adopted orphan who has to learn to **aiteo** of his father and mother in his new home. Before, he had no rights to **aiteo**. Now, having been adopted and given a new surname, he has to learn to **aiteo**. So do we. Do not stay an orphan. If you are born again, you are a son of God and are expected to **aiteo** and have all your needs met by the Father who loves you and has provided the kingdom for you to enjoy.

There are many scriptures that refer to 'asking' and now, as we read them, they should make much more sense. Previously, you may have thought that these scriptures did not make sense as there are few or no conditions to the promises. At least in the Old Testament it is clear - God's promises are conditional. If I obey His laws, including the 10 commandments, then I can expect His blessing. If I do not, I am cursed and suffer the consequences of my disobedience. Then Jesus came and the only condition now is that I believe; believe that He has done it, and it is finished. But when we understand that God dealt with man under the Old Covenant with the Law, which Jesus fulfilled perfectly and nailed the ordinances against us to the cross, we can then understand the New Covenant is by grace alone. He has done it all and we just need to believe. Simple really, but this takes the constant renewing of our minds for it to settle into our hearts as a reality. We know we have it, when our prayers are ones of **aiteo** instead of **erotao**. (I must add a clarification here as only some of our prayers are **aiteo**, or kingly prayers. Later in the book we will deal with priestly prayers which are supplication rather than kingly commands.)

Let us look at some other scriptures using **erotao** and **aiteo**.

John 16:26 *In that day you will **aiteo** in My name, and I do not say to you that I shall **erotao*** (pray) *the Father for you.*

This is a clear instruction from the Lord and we are to ask the Father according to our covenant rights. After the cross He was instructing the disciples that no longer would He pray to the Father for them. They would have direct access to the Father.

John 15:7 *If you abide in Me and My words abide in you, you will **aiteo** what you desire and it will be done for you.*

John 14:12-14 *Most assuredly, I say to you, he who believes in Me, the works that I do he will do also; and greater works than these he will do, because I go to My Father. And whatever you **aiteo** in My name, that I will do, that the Father may be glorified in the Son. If you **aiteo** anything in My name, I will do it.*

This is an astonishing scripture. It seems incredible that we can do the works of Jesus and greater. Immediately after saying this, Jesus showed us how we can do His works - by believing and calling upon our covenant with **aiteo**. Then, by the Holy Spirit, He will do it through us.

Matt 18:19 *Again I say to you that if two of you agree on earth concerning anything that they **aiteo**, it will be done for them by My Father in heaven.*

Matt 21:21-22 *Assuredly, I say to you, if you have faith and do not doubt, you will not only do what was done to that fig tree, but also if you say to this mountain, 'Be removed and be cast into the sea,' it will be done. And whatever things you **aiteo** in prayer, believing, you will receive.*

No mountain of sickness or any other thing that Jesus paid for on the cross can resist the **aiteo** of a believer. It has to go.

Mark 11:23-24 *For assuredly, I say to you, whoever says to this mountain, 'Be removed and be cast into the sea,' and does not doubt in his heart, but believes that those things he says will be done, he will have whatever he says. Therefore, I say to you, whatever things you **aiteo*** *when you pray, believe that you receive them, and you will have them.*

This classic faith scripture is so important in getting answers to our prayers. Note that we have to **aiteo** out loud. We have to pray out loud and verbalise our prayer when asking for things and for circumstances to change. We have to make a kingly declaration. Silent praying may have a place in quiet contemplation and worship, but we will have no results to our kingly prayer unless, from a heart of belief, we declare and claim the promise - **aiteo** it.

Luke 11:9-13 *So I say to you, **aiteo**, and it will be given to you; seek and you will find; knock and it will be opened to you. For everyone who **aiteo** receives, and he who seeks finds, and to him who knocks it will be opened. If a son **aiteo** for bread from any father among you, will he give him a stone? Or if he **aiteo** for a fish, will he give him a serpent instead of a fish? Or if he **aiteo** for an egg, will he offer a scorpion? If you then, being evil, know how to give good gifts to your children, how much more will your heavenly Father give the Holy Spirit to those who **aiteo** Him!*

Like my example of a son asking his mother for food, Jesus is drawing the same parallel between earthly fathers and our heavenly Father. What a sublime promise that if we **aiteo** the Father, we can receive any promise made by the Lord in the book of the covenant, the Bible. And the best gift of all, the Holy Spirit, is promised to us if we just **aiteo**.

Eph 3:20 *Now to Him who is able to do exceedingly, abundantly above all that we **aiteo** or think, according to the power that works in us, to Him be the glory in the church by Christ Jesus to all generations, forever and ever. Amen.*

How superlative is the Father's supply into our every need. We cannot even comprehend how great God's provision for us is, and even above all we can ask (**aiteo**), God's supply will surpass this. All we have to do is approach Him on the basis of our covenant. That is all. Begging and pleading **erotao** will get us nowhere. Our approach has to be through the cross and not according to the need. This is an important point to make here. There is a bottomless pit of needs in this world and our Father cannot respond to any of them without His saints praying and acting in faith.

James 1:5-6 *If any of you lack wisdom, let him **aiteo** of God, who gives liberally, and without reproach, and it will be given to him. But let him **aiteo** in faith, without doubting, for he who doubts is like a wave of the sea driven and tossed by the wind. For let not that man suppose that he will receive anything from the Lord.*

We can add wisdom to all the promises listed above that we can **aiteo.** We cannot receive anything from the Lord unless we are sure of our covenant rights and appropriate them in **aiteo.**

James 4:2-3 *You lust and do not have. You murder and covet and cannot obtain. You fight and war. Yet you do not have because you do not **aiteo.** You **aiteo** and do not* *receive, because you **aiteo** amiss, that you may spend it on your pleasures.*

This is a very powerful scripture reiterating that unless we ask according to our covenant promises, we will receive nothing from God. The Lord promises us that we will be blessed, but this is not so that we can consume it on ourselves; we are blessed to be a blessing to others. God wants us to have all our needs met so that we can show the love of God to others in the blessing we can bestow on them. If we are poor, how can we meet a financial need in someone else, and how can we go and preach the gospel if we are too poor to pay for fuel and maintenance for the vehicle we want to travel in.

1 John 3:22 *And whatever we **aiteo** we receive from Him, because we keep His commandments and do those things that are pleasing in His sight.*

1 John 5:14-15 *Now this is the confidence that we have in Him, that if we **aiteo** anything according to His will, He hears us. And if we know that He hears us, whatever we **aiteo**, we know that we have the petitions that we have **aiteo** of Him.*

As we come to the end of this chapter, we should burn this last scripture into our memory and constantly remember it when we are in prayer. Knowing our covenant position with the Lord enables us to have great confidence that our prayers will be answered. It gives the Lord great joy to see us appropriating all that He died for.

PATTERN IN THE HEAVENS

Augustine once said about scripture: "In the Old Testament the New is concealed; in the New is the Old revealed". The Old Testament is a valuable resource for us that describes our origins and the many natural patterns God has built into Hebrew life. Many of these patterns hold spiritual truths which Jesus would demonstrate and teach in the gospel accounts. The Psalms and the prophets foretold the New Covenant realities that Jesus would establish in His blood on the cross, which was a great mystery to the Old Testament saints.

A pattern and shadow in the Old Testament that is essential for us to understand, is the Tabernacle in the wilderness. Moses was instructed to build the Tabernacle in accordance with the heavenly pattern, in which God hid many New Covenant truths.

Ex 26:30 *And you shall raise up the tabernacle according to its pattern which you were shown on the mountain.*

This pattern shown to Moses, was not new, but was based on the Tabernacle already in heaven.

Heb 9:22-24 *And according to the law almost all things are purified with blood, and without shedding of blood there is no remission. Therefore it was necessary that the copies of the things in the heavens should be purified with these, but the heavenly things themselves with better sacrifices than these. For Christ has not entered the holy places made with hands, which are copies of the true, but into heaven itself, now to appear in the presence of God for us.*

As a shadow of marvellous things to come, the high priest took the blood from the sacrifice and cleansed the furniture in the Tabernacle and offered it upon the mercy seat of the ark of the covenant for the sins of the Israelites, dealing with sin for a year. As foretold in this ritual, Jesus took His perfect blood shed on the cross and cleansed the Tabernacle in heaven and offered His blood on the Mercy Seat before God, once and for all, sanctifying us from sin - past, present and future.

Hidden in the layout of the Tabernacle are truths that pertain to our New Covenant prayer life, and although we do not have the time to go into it fully, I do want to look at the furniture and activities that happened in the Holy Place. The Tabernacle was divided into three sections: the large Outer Court, which all Israelites were allowed into; the much smaller Holy Place which only the Levitical priests were allowed into; the Holy of Holies which only the high priest was allowed into once a year, to offer the sacrificial blood of atonement. God came down in a cloud and dwelt with His people in the Holy of Holies and because of sin, no man could enter His presence. The Holy of Holies was separated from the Holy Place by a very thick curtain. In the Holy Place, in front of the veil, was the Altar of Incense. Incense continually filled this space and protected the high priest once a year on the day of atonement when he went in before God to offer the blood of the sacrifice.

All the items of furniture in the Tabernacle were specially constructed with specific materials as they were a pattern of what was to come in the New Covenant through Jesus. In the Holy Place, the Table of Showbread speaks of the life-giving Word of God. The seven branched menorah gives the only light in the Holy Place and speaks of the revelation that the Holy Spirit brings. The altar of incense speaks of prayer and worship constantly going up before God.

Rev 5:8b *And golden bowls full of incense, which are the prayers of the saints.*

I am so encouraged when I discover confirmations of our faith hidden in the Old Testament. Our belief in Jesus is not something that man concocted, like the empty rituals of the religions of the world. Line upon line, God has laid out truths for us to discover in the Bible. I see the same patterns in the many aspects of prayer hidden in the Word. There are no superfluous details in the Bible. Every detail has its place and purpose. I hope to shed light on more of these details to encourage you in the vitality of our pursuit of God in prayer.

One important detail of the Tabernacle that deserves exploring now, is the thick curtain that separated the Holy Place from the Holy of Holies. It separated the priests serving in the Holy Place from the presence of God in the Holy of Holies. No man could come into God's presence because of sin, and the thick veil was there to protect the priests. This all changed on the day when Jesus died on the cross.

Matt 27:51 *Then, behold, the veil of the temple was torn in two from top to bottom.*

Since the veil in the temple was very thick it was impossible for it to have torn naturally. It had to be God who ripped the veil in two, destroying the separation between man and God in a very dramatic way. Access to God was now freely available to all believers in Christ. Interestingly, the author of Hebrews penned a different arrangement of the furniture in the Holy Place.

Heb 9:2-4a *For a Tabernacle was prepared: the first part, in which was the lampstand, the table, and the showbread, which is called the sanctuary* (Holy Place)*; and behind the second veil, the part of the Tabernacle which is called the Holiest of All* (Holy of Holies), *which had the golden censer* (altar of incense) *and the ark of the covenant.*

In this passage, the altar of incense is in the Holy of Holies. In the wilderness, this could not have been so, because the priests could not have had access to it to recharge the coals and the incense. In the Hebrews account, the altar of incense is in the Holy of Holies because the veil had been torn and removed and the altar of incense was now in front of the ark of the covenant. Our prayers and worship go unimpeded into the presence of God. This is a wonderful picture of an important difference between the Old and New Covenants.

PAUL'S PRAYERS

In a previous chapter, we saw that to effect change in our circumstances, we demand of our covenant, commanding change in a kingly manner. There is another category of prayer that I have called priestly prayer.

In areas where we have authority, for instance, over our own bodies, in our homes, in our finances and in our businesses, we can pray kingly prayers. We can **aiteo** to change the circumstances and to ask for things for ourselves. But when we want to pray for others, we cannot **aiteo**. We do not have authority over their lives, and we have to pray in a priestly way. We ask of the Father by the agency of the Holy Spirit, to bring change in a person's life.

All those years ago, preparing for my Bible school class on prayer, I was captivated by the beautiful way in which Paul wrote his prayers for the saints in the churches he had planted. He gave us a template for priestly prayer for people we care about, and even for leaders that we might not care much about but desire a change in their lives as they rule over us.

As we will see in a later chapter, the most effective way we can pray priestly prayers is by praying the scriptures. If we are praying the Word, we cannot do better than praying Paul's prayers.

The most powerful and comprehensive prayers of Paul are in Eph 1:16-23 and Eph 3:14-21. Paul is praying for the church in Ephesus, and what we can do is personalise his prayers for the person we want to pray for. As we do this, Paul's prayer becomes our prayer, and we find that we can expand certain parts of our prayer for the specific needs of the individual we are praying for. Paul's prayers provide a substantial framework for our own specific prayers.

Let us take Eph 1:17-23 and I will personalise it for one of my sons, Stephen:

"I pray that the God of our Lord Jesus Christ, the Father of glory, may give Stephen the spirit of wisdom and revelation in the knowledge of You in all the decisions he makes for his family and business. May the eyes of Stephen's understanding be enlightened that he may know the hope of Your calling for him, always giving the pre-eminence to You as he builds his business. May Stephen come to know that his temporal and eternal reward is dependent on the way he treats people, letting the love of Christ always flow through him. May the Word, that I know is firmly planted in Stephen's heart, be powerful and effective in his life in all circumstances. Amen."

Eph 3:16-21 is another powerful prayer. For example, you can pray:

"That You, Lord Jesus, would grant my friend (insert their name) to be strengthened with might through Your Spirit in his/her inner man, and that Christ may dwell in his/her heart through faith. That he/she, being rooted and grounded in love, may be able to comprehend what is the width and length and depth and height, and to know the love of Christ, which passes knowledge, that he/she may be filled with all the fullness of God. Amen."

The application of these prayers is limitless and help us to stay within the framework of priestly prayer. We should never stray and pray controlling prayers where we want to impose our will upon someone else. These prayers will not be answered, as even God will not override our free choice.

I was so taken by these prayers that I asked my Bible school students to choose one of Paul's Ephesian prayers to memorise, and they were required to write it out in an exam. Many grumbled but I know that there is nothing better than having the Word hidden in one's heart, that can be pulled out when needed. Recently, I met a former Bible school student who said that although she had found it hard at the time, she is now very grateful for the prayers she learnt, and more importantly, the value of hiding the Word in her heart. On another occasion, a couple who had both attended my prayer class at Bible school said that they can still recite the two prayers they had asked to memorise from Ephesians. After 39 years, they both remembered the Greek words for 'ask', **aiteo** and **erotao**. I was so blessed to hear them say that.

There are many of Paul's prayers that we can pray as a priest of our God. Below are the prayers that I have found in Paul's writings:

Rom 15:13 *Now may the God of hope fill you with all joy and peace in believing, that you may abound in hope by the power of the Holy Spirit.*

Rom 15:31-32 *that I may be delivered from those ... who do not believe, and that my service ... may be acceptable to the saints, that I may come to you with joy by the will of God, and may be refreshed together with you.*

1 Cor 1:4-8 *I thank my God always concerning you for the grace of God which was given to you by Christ Jesus, that you were enriched in everything by Him in all utterance and all knowledge, even as the testimony of Christ was confirmed in you, so that you come short in no gift, eagerly waiting for the revelation of our Lord Jesus Christ, who will also confirm you to the end that you may be blameless in the day of our Lord Jesus Christ.*

2 Cor 1:11 *you also helping together in prayer for us, that thanks may be given by many persons on our behalf for the gift granted to us through many.*

2 Cor 13:7,9 *Now I pray to God that you do no evil ... that you should do what is honourable ... For we are glad when we are weak and you are strong. And this we also pray, that you may be made complete.*

Eph 6:19 *and for me, that utterance may be given to me, that I may open my mouth boldly to make known the mystery of the gospel.*

Phil 1:9-11 *And this I pray, that your love may abound yet more and more in knowledge and all discernment, that you may approve the things which are excellent, that you may be sincere and without offense till the day of Christ, being filled with the fruits of righteousness which are by Christ Jesus, to the glory and praise of God.*

Col 1:9-11a *that you may be filled with the knowledge of His will in all wisdom and spiritual understanding; that you may walk worthy of the Lord, fully pleasing Him, being fruitful in every good work and increasing in the knowledge of God, strengthened with all might.*

Col 4:3-4 *praying* also for us, *that God would open to us a door for the word, to speak the mystery of Christ ... that I may make it manifest as I ought to speak.*

Col 4:12b *that you may stand perfect and complete in all the will of God.*

1 Thess 3:12-13a *And may the Lord make you increase and abound in love to one another and to all ... so that He may establish your hearts blameless in holiness before our God and Father.*

2 Thess 1:11-12 *Therefore we also pray always for you that our God would count you worthy of this calling, and fulfil all the good pleasure of His goodness and the work of faith with power, that the name of our Lord Jesus Christ may be glorified in you, and you in Him, according to the grace of our God and the Lord Jesus Christ.*

2 Thess 3:1-2 *Finally, brethren, pray for us that the word of the Lord may run swiftly and be glorified, just as it is*

with you, and that we may be delivered from unreasonable and wicked men; for not all have faith.

Philemon 1:6 *that the sharing of your faith may become effective by the acknowledgement of every good thing which is in you in Christ Jesus.*

As you can see, Paul was prolific in writing down his prayers for the saints. I only found one non-Pauline prayer recorded in the epistles:

3 John 1:2 *Beloved, I pray that you may prosper in all things and be in health, just as your soul prospers.*

From Paul's prayers we can pray a broad spread of subjects over people, including: knowledge, understanding, seeing, hope, calling, riches, glory, inheritance, power, revelation, overcoming, strength, love, joy, peace, refreshing, generosity, deliverance from evil men, acceptable service, being blameless, doing no evil, doing honourable things, utterance given, boldness, being without offense, showing fruits of righteousness, walking worthy, doing good works, for God to open a door, to speak the mystery of the gospel, to stand perfect and complete and that the Word may spread swiftly.

Paul has penned a superb resource for us to use in prayer, covering most aspects of our daily lives. Let us use his words and show our love for the Lord and His people by praying as priests, effectively and often.

Prayers Stored as Incense

It is God's desire for us to always contend in prayer for our families. Paul said in Rom 1:9 *without ceasing I make mention of you always in my prayers.* Our prayers never go to waste. There is a lovely picture in Revelation that shows what happens to our prayers in the presence of God.

Rev 5:8 *Now when He had taken the scroll, the four living creatures and the twenty-four elders fell down before the Lamb, each having a harp, and golden bowls* (vials in KJV) *full of incense, which are the prayers of the saints.*

Some scholars say that these prayers are of the martyrs under the throne, asking for vengeance. But I believe that this heavenly picture is bigger than being just about the prayers of the martyrs stored in vials until they are poured out during the tribulation. Our words, especially when we pray the Word of God, are spirit and they contain life and when they cannot be applied straight away, I believe that they are stored in bowls or vials and poured out when the time is right.

David describes a similar scene of his prayers going up as incense to the Lord.

Ps 141:2 *Let my prayer be set before You as incense, the lifting up of my hands as the evening sacrifice.*

So, we should not be discouraged when we do not see anything happening in response to our prayers. Keep on praying and standing in faith for the solution. The precious prayers, prayed according to the principles that we are discussing in this book, are kept to be poured out at the perfect time. Never give up, even if it takes years, or even decades. Our prayers may be stored up to be poured out for our great grandchildren and even in generations beyond, long after we have gone to be with the Lord.

FIRST OF ALL

In 1 Tim 2:1-2, Paul encourages Timothy by saying *first of all that supplications, prayers, intercessions and giving of thanks be made for all men, for kings and all who are in authority, that we may lead a quiet and peaceful life in all godliness and reverence.*

Prov 29:2 *When the righteous are in authority, the people rejoice; but when the wicked man rules, the people groan.*

Our words have great power, which we will discuss in another chapter. We will have what we say. If all we do is complain and criticize the government of the day, we do not improve the situation. Paul instructs us to pray FOR those in authority. We can pray some of Paul's prayers in the epistles for those in authority over us, and then the Holy Spirit and the angels can bring positive influence over the rulers. The angels' actions are restricted if we speak negative words over the authorities.

The kingdom of darkness exerts an insidious influence in many countries where a large amount of worship is to ancestors and to demons. This strengthens evil power over the leaders, and wicked men with unrighteous intentions rise and take prominent positions of authority. The prayers of the saints will confuse the plans of the devil and the people under his influence, and righteous men will be strengthened and take courage to stand up to the evil around them.

All too often we are carnal in our outlook, only seeing the temporal things that our senses can see and hear. But these pass away in time and the unseen realm is far more important because it is eternal.

2 Cor 4:18 *while we do not look at the things which are seen, but at the things which are not seen. For the things which are seen are temporary, but the things which are not seen are eternal.*

A spiritual war rages around us that we cannot see. Forces of evil take every opportunity to effect their plans of killing, stealing and destroying, and they are strengthened by negative words, and have direct influence in our world through unregenerate hearts. Conversely, the forces of good are released and even commissioned by God's people who know how to speak positive words of the Lord into the circumstances around them. These men of God **aiteo** and change negative situations around them for good, and the priests of God pray for people, and especially those in authority, to rise up and act righteously.

Paul tells Timothy why we should pray for those in authority. He says in 1 Tim 2:2-4 that not only will we *lead a quiet and peaceable life in all godliness and reverence,* but also that *our God and Saviour desires that all men to be saved and come to the knowledge of the truth.*

You may say, "are we just to turn the other cheek and let these evil corrupt people get away with it?" We should not ignore the actions of evil people, but we should not make it worse by acting carnally. Paul encourages us to act spiritually, knowing that there is a spiritual war that we are involved in and the only way to make a positive change is to pray. Physical action can follow, but prayer FOR leaders must go first. There will be a time to stand for election, to protest and to make your voice heard, to support a political party and, of course, to vote. But do the first thing first and continue to do it - pray for those in authority.

Many years ago, I remember praying with a church group in Harare, and one man was praying against the people of the ruling party. It jarred within my spirit as he prayed that these evil men be destroyed. When I questioned him, he justified his prayer by pointing to David and his prayers in Psalms. "Look", he said, "see how David prayed for his enemies to be destroyed." This is called precatory prayer, and some justify their negative prayer by the way David prayed. I argued with this man that after the cross, we cannot pray this type of prayer anymore. Paul instructed Timothy to pray FOR all men. At no time in the New Testament are we instructed to pray precatory prayers.

Prayer Power in Persia

There is a great example of the power of prayer to influence the ruler in the book of Esther. Evil Haman had persuaded King Ahasuerus to issue a decree whereby on a specific date, all the people of the kingdom were to kill the Jews and confiscate their property. Queen Esther, a Jew, was warned by her uncle, Mordecai, that even she as a Jew would die because of this evil decree. Mordecai pleaded with her to intercede with the king for her people. Esther agreed to Mordecai's plan, and bravely accepted the task. But she knew she could not be successful without God's help. So, she instructed Mordecai to *Go gather all the Jews who are present in Shushan, and fast for me; neither eat or drink for three days, night or day. My maids and I will fast likewise. And so I will go to the king, which is against the law; and if I perish, I perish!* (Esther 4:16).

As they fasted, the Jews prayed, and God was able to put a plan into action to save His people. Esther did her part which was to have the king attend a banquet and to invite evil Haman. Not only did God give Esther favour with the king, but He added a vital ingredient to the deliverance plan; to have Mordecai honoured and to have Haman show him off to the whole city. In Esther chapter 6 we see that God disturbed the sleep of the king and gave him the idea to review the chronicles of the kingdom. He read of the acts of Mordecai in which he had exposed a treasonous plot against the king, yet had not been rewarded. So, the next day, in an ironic twist, Haman was instructed to parade Mordecai through the city and to honour him. You can read the rest of the story yourself to see how Haman fell into his own trap and was hanged on the gallows on which he intended to hang Mordecai. Fervent prayer by all the Jews caused favour to be upon Esther and Mordecai, and the Lord was able to save the entire nation. The Jews knew that their salvation could only come from the Lord, and therefore, they humbled themselves and prayed. The Lord was able to deliver His people from an impossible situation. He is in the same business today if we will trust Him and pray.

When we pray, we enable the Holy Spirit and the angels to work out a solution for us, even to influencing the king in ways beyond our understanding of the big picture and of the solution that is needed. Similarly, our leaders can make positive decisions for the nation if we will pray FOR them.

Prov 21:1 *The king's heart is in the hand of the Lord. Like the rivers of water: He turns it wherever He wishes.*

So, let us pray FOR those in authority, even if we think that they are evil. Jesus instructed us in Matt 5:44 to *love your enemies, bless those that curse you, do good to those that hate you, and pray for those who spitefully use you and persecute you.*

I struggle with the use of a very well-known scripture in praying for our nation.

2 Chron 7:14 *If My people who are called by My name will humble themselves, and pray and seek My face, and turn from their wicked ways, then I will hear from heaven, and I will forgive their sin and heal their land.*

The first part of this scripture is great. We are called by His name, and it is good to humble ourselves and pray and seek His face. But this scripture says that God hearing our prayer is conditional on us turning from our wicked ways. In 1 John 5:14-15 we are told that we can have confidence that He hears our prayer, and we have the answers we seek, and the only condition is that we

aiteo according to His will. In our New Covenant, God has already forgiven our sins and He has positionally healed our land. He has already done all that He will ever do. He cried out on the cross *"It is finished!"* Better than using 2 Chron 7:14 as our guide on how to pray, is to use 2 Tim 2:1. People have to repent of their own sin in order for them to receive forgiveness. We cannot do it for them.

There is a plethora of prayers that we can pray out of the Psalms alone. For example, Psalm 33 is full of material for us to pray for our nation.

We can proclaim prophetically that *the earth is full of the goodness of the Lord* (v5) and *The Lord brings the counsel of the nations to nothing; He makes the plans of the peoples of no effect. The counsel of the Lord stands forever, the plans of His heart to all generations. Blessed is the nation whose God is the Lord* (v10-12). Then we can pray *Let Your mercy, O Lord, be upon us, just as we hope in You* (v22).

South African Salvation

Evidence of the power of prayer for a nation can be seen in the events that resulted in the first majority rule election in South Africa in 1994. It ended the apartheid system, and the run up to elections was fraught with seemingly impossible barriers to a smooth transition. Bloody clashes and political infighting threatened to derail the whole process ... But God! Christians prayed, like never before, and some very influential Christian leaders were involved in the political process. One such leader was Micheal

Cassidy, the founder of Africa Enterprise. His book, 'A Witness Forever', describes how the Lord led South Africa through a peaceful transition, and spared the country from civil war that was predicted to be the worst bloodbath that Africa had ever seen. Cassidy was instrumental in getting the main political players in the election process, to dialogue. It is commonly believed that Mandela, de Klerk, Buthelezi and the other leaders would never have found a place of compromise of their polar positions on government, without the people of God praying. The peaceful transition to majority rule in 1994 could not have happened without the intervention of the Lord, and that could not have happened without the prayers of the saints.

I believe that we saw another outpouring of prayer 30 years later, leading up to the 2024 South African general elections. At the ballot box, both nationally and provincially, the corrupt ruling party of 30 years, lost its majority and was forced to form a Government of National Unity. We are thrilled to see God continuing to bring positive changes in South Africa through His people, as Christians continue to pray for their leaders.

The Christmas scripture in Is 9:6-7 should motivate us to continue praying for our leaders *... and the government will be upon His shoulder ... Of the increase of His government and peace there will be no end.*

KEYS OF THE KINGDOM

Matt 16:19 *And I will give you the keys of the kingdom of heaven, and whatever you bind on earth will be bound in heaven, and whatever you loose on earth will be loosed in heaven.*

What a powerful scripture! Jesus said this right after Peter recognised Jesus as the Son of God, and Jesus said in verse 18 that *on this rock* (of the revelation of Jesus as the Son of God) *I will build My church, and the gates of Hades shall not prevail against it.* The next word is 'And' at the beginning of verse 19. This means that the revelation of Jesus Christ is the foundation upon which His Church is being built. As Christians we should be ruling and reigning through the keys of binding and loosing that we have been given, defeating the plans of the devil and his evil schemes. I do not think that we really grasp the significance of this statement from our commander in chief. If we understand our covenant rights in the Kingdom of God, we can speak as kings on this earth, and whatever blessing we release (loose) will be backed by heaven. Whatever demonic force and influence we bar (bind), the full authority of heaven stands behind our words.

To open the doors of our houses, we need keys. We need to get into the house through the door to have the benefit of everything inside - provision, shelter and security.

Similarly, we access the benefits of the kingdom by using the keys which have been given to us when we are born again and have renewed our minds to the stunning power that can be unleashed on the earth through our words. We will explore the power of our words in a later chapter.

Jesus expands His instructions to us two chapters later in Matt 18:18. It follows His instructions on how to deal with a brother who sins against us. Firstly, we go to him and tell him his fault. If he hears us, then we have gained our brother. If he does not, take another brother, and through two witnesses, try to reconcile. If he refuses to hear you both, then we are to tell the church and have the whole body admonish him. If he does not come around and repent, then we are to treat him as *a heathen and tax collector*. In other words, we refuse to fellowship with him and deny him the benefits and protection of the church. Hopefully, he will come to himself and repent. In the next verse, Jesus says *Assuredly, I say to you* (ie this is a fundamental important truth), *whatever you bind on earth will be bound in heaven, and whatever you loose on earth will be loosed in heaven*. I interpret this to say that the blessing released by our words upon the saints in the church is very powerful and we are to hold back the blessing of our prayers from an unrepentant person. If we continue to pray for him as if he was not sinning, then it will be difficult for him to come to himself and realise what he has done is wrong. We should pray for him as if he was an unbeliever, far from God. This priestly kind of prayer would be along the lines of 2 Cor 4:6, where we are asking for God to command the light to shine in his darkened mind and heart, to give him the light of the knowledge of the glory of God which will deliver him from his deception. The god of this age, the devil, has blinded him, so that he does not believe and therefore, will not repent. Our priestly prayer releases the Holy Spirit to work in his heart and bring a change. Also, we can bind the work of the devil who is blinding the understanding of the brother or sister so they cannot see or understand their sin.

It seems that Paul did a similar thing with Hymenaeus and Alexander in 1 Tim 1:20 where he handed them over to Satan so they could learn not to blaspheme. It seems that he loosed the power of the devil over these men as they were dangerous to the church, and he bound the blessing and covering of the church from protecting them. The church would have been instructed not to pray for them as brothers but treat them as unbelievers and pray for them according to 2 Cor 4:4,6. This demonstrates the huge authority and responsibility we have as believers, and reminds us that we cannot slip into prayers that try to control people to conform them to our will, however well intended. Furthermore, this drastic measure of handing a brother over to Satan is not something done lightly, and it is a matter for the elders of the church to do after exhausting all other measures to get the brother or sister to repent.

John 20:23 *If you forgive sins of any, they are forgiven them; if you retain the sins of any, they are retained.*

This is an astounding scripture. Jesus was telling us that we can loose and bind sins. With the grace of the Lord Jesus Christ in our mouths, we can address those that are bound by the devil and tell them that their sins are forgiven. This is not just the privilege of a bishop or priest; it is for all believers. How liberating it is for us to speak over an unbeliever that the kingdom has come to him and that his sins are forgiven!

Prayer of Agreement

Matt 18:19-20 *Again I say to you that if two of you agree on earth concerning anything that they **aiteo**, it will be done for them by My Father in heaven.*

Agreement in prayer is very powerful, especially in a marriage. This is one of the reasons why the devil works to bring strife between a husband and a wife. If he can bring disharmony between them, they will be hampered from loosing blessing over their children, and from binding the devil's activities against them.

1 Peter 3:7 *Husbands, likewise, dwell with them* (wives) *with understanding, giving honour to the wife, as to the weaker vessel, and as being heirs together of the grace of life, that your prayers may not be hindered.*

God's grace is poured out over the couple to enable them to do life together and to be powerful in prayer as they agree and pray according to their covenant for their family.

The devil has no answer for prayers of agreement, as well as prayers of binding and loosing, spoken by Christians submitted to God and fully cognisant of their covenant rights in Christ. That is why Jesus said in Matt 16:18 that *the gates of Hades shall not prevail against it* (the Church). If a brother or family member is captive to sin, pray in agreement according to your covenant rights, and the devil has to let them go. We have the keys, and he is defeated by the blood of the Lamb.

Key of David

There is another powerful key that is spoken of in the Bible, and that is the key of David. Beautiful imagery is attached to this key for New Covenant believers.

Is 22:22 *The key of the house of David I will lay on his shoulder; So he shall open, and no one shall shut; And he shall shut, and no one shall open.*

The context of this scripture is that Isaiah was prophesying against a steward called Shebna. The Lord will *toss you like a ball ...* and *drive you out of your office ... Then it shall be in that day, that I will call My servant Eliakim, the son of Hilkiah ... I will commit your responsibility into his hand. He shall be a father to the inhabitants of Jerusalem and to the house of Judah* (Is 22:18-21).

Shebna's position was to be given to Eliakim to be the steward over the king's household. This was an important position, the highest in the royal household. As such,

Eliakim had the authority to admit people into the presence of the king. Only through Eliakim could the people get an audience with King David. If he shut the door, there was no way anyone could have an audience with the king.

Before we go on, let us look at another scripture on the key of David.

Rev 3:7-8 *And to the angel of the church in Philadelphia write, 'These things says He who is holy, He who is true, "He who has the key of David, He who opens and no one shuts, and shuts and no one opens": "I know your works. See, I have set before you an open door, and no one can shut it".*

In this scripture, it is Jesus who holds the key of David, controlling access to His kingdom. Because the Philadelphians' works were good, they are shown an open door of access, favour and blessing in the kingdom, and no one can impede that access. As Jesus has delegated authority to His saints on the earth, I do not think it is a stretch of the truth to say that we have been given the key of David to open the door for people to gain access to the kingdom. We have been given the ministry of reconciliation (2 Cor 5:18) and we are to preach the gospel of grace to the lost and show them the way of salvation.

Like Eliakim, we have been given the keys to the kingdom, and through prayer, we open the door and clear the way for the lost or the backslidden to come into the kingdom. In prayer, we pray that the soil of the hearts of the disobedient be prepared, so that they can receive the word of reconciliation and be saved. As we have seen, we have the key of the kingdom to bind evil forces impeding people from receiving the gospel, and if we open the door for them in prayer, no one can shut it.

We can also use the key of David in our lives as we pray for opportunities to open for us in ministry, and in any other area of our lives. We can pray scripture and pray in the Spirit for a door to open for us, and we can resist the devil from shutting down the opportunity and closing the door by binding him in authoritative prayer.

Another application of the scripture in Isaiah 22, can be seen in Romans 11. Paul is talking about the natural olive branches being broken off and the wild olive branches being grafted in. The Jews rejected Christ in unbelief and so were 'tossed out' like Shebna. We, like Eliakim, have been grafted into the household of God and the Church now holds the key of David to reconcile the world back to God. We are warned in Rom 11:20b-22 *Do not be haughty, but fear. For if God did not spare the natural branches, He may not spare you either. Therefore consider the goodness and severity of God: on those who fell, severity; but towards you, goodness, if you continue in His goodness. Otherwise, you also will be cut off.*

Paul is not saying that we can lose our eternal salvation like this, but if we count the goodness of the Lord a light thing, and ignore His commandments, we will be cut off from the life-giving sap from the vine and our spiritual lives will shrivel. We should continue in seeking Him, abiding in the vine (a condition to our answered **aiteo**), and praying for His kingdom to come on earth as it is in heaven.

PRAYING THE WORD

The deeper we explore the subject of prayer, the more we realise the magnificent power of our words. In the beginning, the words of God created the heavens and the earth and everything in it. The Word of God came to earth and was born a man and turned the world right side up by declaring the truth about the Father and His purpose on the earth.

When we believe and accept the covenant that Jesus cut for us on the cross, we are transformed into another being; born again as sons of God, empowered by His Spirit to do His works and greater works on the earth and to bring heaven to earth.

We can only do this by ruling according to His words, and not ours. God's words have been written for us in the Bible so we can speak them out to change the circumstances around us. The written Word is the *logos,* the general revelation of God for man. When that *logos* is activated by the Holy Spirit and applied to a specific person in a specific situation for a specific time, the *logos* becomes the *rhema* of God.

We find this transformation from *logos* to *rhema* hidden in a verse in Luke. The angel Gabriel appeared to Mary, and he announced to her that she would become pregnant by the Holy Spirit and that her relative, Elizabeth, who had been barren, was six months pregnant.

Luke 1:37 *For with God nothing will be impossible.*

I think the Bible translators had great difficulty with this verse as the word translated as 'nothing' in the Greek is actually 'no rhema'. So, no *rhema* will be impossible. That is so powerful! The seed of the *logos* was planted in Mary by the Holy Spirit, and it became a specific word at a specific time - a *rhema*. Every *rhema* will come to pass.

This means that as we hide the Word of God, the *logos*, in our hearts, the Holy Spirit will quicken the right word at the right time and when we **aiteo** the *rhema*, it has to come to pass.

There is another agency that swings into operation when we declare the *rhema* of God.

Ps 103:20 *Bless the Lord, you His angels, who excel in strength, who do His word, heeding the voice of His word.*

According to this scripture, the angels are waiting to hear the Word of God spoken from our mouths. Then they are tasked with bringing our **aiteo** to pass.

Eph 6:17b *and the sword of the Spirit, which is the word of God.*

The Word of God in our mouths is like a sword in the spirit. When we speak the Word of God, it is energised by the Holy Spirit and we know that every Word of God we speak will *not return to Me void, but it shall accomplish what I please, and it shall prosper in the thing for which I sent it* (Is 55:11).

It is important to note that we are instructed in these scriptures to pray the Word of God and not our words. I am sure you have been to prayer meetings where people pray long prayers informing God of all the trials and tribulations of their lives, as if He was unaware. God knows our needs before we even ask. A better use of our prayer time would be to declare the promises of God, confident that He is able to change every negative circumstance we face.

If we have a need for something, then we should find the scripture that describes our covenant right to that thing, and **aiteo** the covenant word. It needs to be a *rhema* word that has been quickened to your heart by the Holy Spirit, that is real to you. If we see a need in another person, then we should pray the Word of God in a priestly manner over the person.

If we do not know the specifics of the person's need, we should pray in tongues for them. This is a perfect way of praying God's will for people, and we will expand on this in another chapter.

Prayer of Faith

James 5:14-15 *Is anyone among you sick? Let him call for the elders of the church, and let them pray over him, anointing him with oil in the name of the Lord. And the prayer of faith will save the sick, and the Lord will raise him up. And if he has committed sins, he will be forgiven.*

This is a very powerful scripture and there is a lot here that I would like to unpack.

I will never forget the time when I was a very young Christian, and the father of a very good friend of mine had just had a heart attack. She called the pastor, and he said he would go to the hospital as soon as he could, and that we must pray the prayer of faith. Panic hit us after finishing the call as we did not know what the prayer of faith was. We could not find the definition in the Bible, so she called the pastor back and asked, "What is the prayer of faith?" He kindly said that we should pray the Word in faith. We could do that, and we did, but the phrase threw us as our understanding of prayer was very rudimentary. We felt very foolish, and I determined to know more about prayer for myself, so I did not have to run to the pastor every time there was a crisis.

As we have already seen, we have to have faith to pray, and the prayer of faith is simply praying the Word in an **aiteo** manner. We declare healing over the sick and do not beg God to heal them. That brings up another point. So often we say that we will pray for the sick and ask God to do something for the person. Why do we ask Jesus to do something that He has already done? Our words and attitude in praying for the sick is often wrong. In Matt 10:8 Jesus instructed the disciples to *heal the sick, cleanse the lepers, raise the dead, cast out demons.* These are commands and Jesus did not tell them to pray for the sick. They were told to heal them. We have the same instruction and that is why our understanding of **aiteo** is vital for us to pray effectively. The only way to heal the sick is to command healing to come into their body as it is their covenant right. Jesus has done it all through the finished work of the cross. The Holy Spirit has provided us with the power to manifest healing through us for the person who is sick. There is nothing wrong with saying that we will pray for healing as long as we know that we will **aiteo** and speak it like a king.

There are a couple of other points I would like to make while we are in James 5:14-15. Firstly, the prayer is said 'in the name of the Lord'. Many times, we tag onto our prayer 'in Jesus' name', usually without thinking. Was James saying that this is an important part of our prayer of faith? I think not. I think it was to emphasise that we need to **aiteo** in our prayer of faith as the covenant that Jesus ratified in His blood is the reason we can pray this way. We should not use 'in Jesus' name' as punctuation at the end of our prayer, but there is nothing wrong with using it if it will help our faith and the sick to receive. As we should already know, we go in the name of the Lord and carry His name as ambassadors. We should not need to tag onto our prayer 'in Jesus' name' to give it more authority.

Secondly, there is the anointing oil mentioned in James 5:14-15. There are two records of oil being used in healing in the New Testament - here in James 5:14 and also in Mark 6:13. Is there anything holy or special about the anointing oil? In the Old Testament, the anointing oil was very special and specially made. But that was a shadow of the Holy Spirit to come, and He is the important part of our prayer, not the oil. So why is it used in healing the sick? The Bible is silent on this, and some Bible teachers believe that it creates a point of contact for the person. They can feel and smell the oil, and their senses can make contact with the unseen and help them receive. The oil is an aid, and not the main thing. Declaring the word of healing over the person will enable the Holy Spirit to manifest healing in the person's body. I will never forget praying for a dear friend many years my senior who was having a lot of pain from his knee prothesis. He came into the meeting on crutches and when we prayed for him, I doused his knee in olive oil. It soaked his trousers, and I apologised for spoiling them with the excessive use of oil. However, he was healed instantly and walked out of the meeting without the aid of his crutches. A week later he told me that he had a healed knee and, surprisingly, all the oil washed out of his trousers.

Like oil, handkerchiefs were used as a point of contact in Acts 19:12. Cloths and aprons were laid on Paul's body and then taken to the sick, and they were healed. There was nothing special about the cloths, but they provided a point of contact.

The final point I want to bring up out of James 5:14-15 *And if he has committed sins, he will be forgiven.* We know that Jesus has paid for our sins, past, present and future, but often sin brings condemnation, and some people may think they cannot be healed if they have sinned. When we pray for them, we need to assure them that their sins are already forgiven, and if necessary, have them pray 1 John 1:9, so that they can receive their healing. Unforgiveness will be a serious barrier for someone seeking healing, and it is important, if unforgiveness is discerned, to have the sick person released from this before declaring healing over them.

The Word is a Seed

In Mark chapter 4, Jesus tells the parable of the sower, and most of us are familiar with the lesson that He was conveying, especially as it was explained in verses 13 to 20. In verse 20 we read that for the Word to be productive in our lives, it has to be planted in a receptive heart.

Mark 4:26-28 *And He said, "The kingdom of God is as if a man should scatter seed on the ground, and should sleep by night and rise by day, and the seed should sprout and grow, he himself does not know how. For the earth yields crops by itself: first the blade, then the head, after that the full grain in the head".*

In the natural, no life exists on earth that has not come from a seed. Spiritually it is the same. We cannot get born again unless the seed of the Word is planted in our heart. Likewise, unless we have the Word in us, in our heart not just in our head in mental assent, it is impossible for us to benefit from the promises of our covenant. There has to be seed in the ground for there to be a harvest. In the parables above, the soil is our heart, and the seed is the Word. It is essential to get the Word into our hearts so it can produce a harvest when we need it. The astonishing thing is, that according to Mark 4:26, the seed grows of itself. We cannot do anything to make a seed grow. Within it there is all that it needs to germinate and grow as long as it has soft, moist soil around it. The same happens in the spirit - plant the Word in a receptive (soft) heart and it will grow. We do not know how it does it, but as we read, contemplate and meditate on the Word, it will grow and mature on its own, and when we need a harvest of healing or any other provision of the New Covenant, the Word in us, mature and ready, will produce the harvest we need.

You may ask, "What about the young Christian who knows nothing about the Word and yet receives healing so easily when prayed for?" God in His grace has made provision for babes in Christ so that they can benefit from the New Covenant promises. A more mature Christian (measured spiritually, not by age) who has faith, can pray for young Christians and **aiteo** healing over them and they shall be healed (James 5:15). We can also pray for unbelievers in the same way. Jesus asked most of those that He healed, "What can I do for you?" He was assessing what Word they had in their hearts, and their level of faith, and He met them at their level. Every person who receives anything from God, has at least the smallest 'mustard' sized faith in their heart to ask for deliverance. That is why we have to preach the gospel as it sows seeds into people's hearts, and if they receive them, they can reap a harvest and be delivered.

The Lord wants us to mature, get the Word into our hearts and grow up in the things of the kingdom. Then we can get healed ourselves by the Word that we have planted in our hearts.

CORRECTLY UNDERSTANDING THE COVENANTS

When we pray the Word of God, we need to be careful of how we pray Old Testament prayers. We have already seen that we cannot pray precatory prayers as David did. Furthermore, many marvellous promises in the Old Testament were conditional, and often do not apply to us as New Testament or New Covenant believers.

Let us review the main covenants described in the Bible before going on, so that we can understand how to pray the Word of God from the different covenants.

Firstly, the Abrahamic covenant was an unconditional covenant in that Abraham had only to believe God at His word. He did not have to do anything.

Then there was the Mosaic covenant or the Law, and here God gave conditional promises to Israel. There are sublime promises made, but all required the Israelites to do their part. They did not need to believe; they had to obey the 10 commandments and keep the plethora of other laws before they could receive the promises.

Many promises in the Old Testament pointed to Jesus coming, and cutting the best and final covenant in His blood on the cross. As He paid the penalty for our sins, and fulfilled all the requirements of the Law, the promises of God are now, once again, conditional on only one thing - that we believe.

Let us look at some of the promises in the three covenants and see how we could pray them.

Abrahamic Covenant

The following three scriptures in Galatians show us that we have the right to claim Abraham's promises:

Gal 3:9 *So then those who are of faith are blessed with believing Abraham.*

Gal 3:13-14 *Christ has redeemed us from the curse of the law, having become a curse for us, for it is written, "Cursed is everyone who hangs on a tree", that the blessing of Abraham might come upon the Gentiles in Christ Jesus, that we might receive the promise of the Spirit through faith.*

Gal 3:29 *And if you are Christ's, then you are Abraham's seed, and heirs according to the promise.*

Abraham's promises are magnificent and wide in their effect. Praying them needs very little adjustment for us today as they are unconditional promises only requiring our belief. Of course, some promises are particular to the coming Christ through Abraham's offspring, and the return of the Jews to the land of Israel, but we can claim the rest of the promises. I have added below short examples of how we can pray using Abraham's promises, and you can expand on them in whatever way is appropriate to your circumstances.

Gen 12:2 *I will bless you … and you shall be a blessing.* We can pray, "Thank you, Lord, that You have blessed

71

me abundantly, not because of my works, but because of what You did for me on the cross. As You bless me, I have an abundance to share with others and I am able to be a blessing to all who You bring across my path". This may be a faith prayer for you as you do not have an abundance right now. But by praying this prayer, we **aiteo** and call upon our covenant to make it so.

Gen 15:1 *Do not be afraid, Abram, I am your shield, your exceedingly great reward.* We can pray, "I declare that I am not afraid of anything or anyone as the Lord is my shield, and He protects me and blesses me". The word 'reward' used here is 'payment for a contract'. So, the Lord promises us that according to our covenant, it is our contractual right to be protected.

Gen 22:17 *blessing I will bless you, and multiplying I will multiply your descendants … and your descendants shall possess the gate of your enemies.* We can pray, "My children and my children's children are blessed in You, Lord, and they are overcomers in all they put their hands to".

Mosaic Covenant

The Mosaic covenant was a conditional covenant; God's blessings on the Israelites were contingent on the Israelites doing something first, in obedience. That was the nature of the Law. So, we must be careful to appropriate these promises in light of our New Covenant.

There is prayer that we can extract out of Deuteronomy 28, full of God's promises for us. However, this scripture was given under the Law, and we need to modify the wording so that it applies to us. I will pray the first part of Deut 28:1-14, below, and personalise it, and you can compare this to the original scripture in your Bible, noting how I have changed the conditions in the scripture to promises so that we can claim them in Christ. For example, by ourselves we cannot perfectly *diligently obey the voice of the Lord your God, to observe carefully all His commandments* (Deut 28:1). Jesus was the only one who could obey God perfectly. So, we rephrase this condition and state that Jesus has obeyed perfectly on our behalf, and therefore, we qualify to receive the promises. Furthermore, as He has already met the conditions when He was on earth, and I am in Him, then I can prophetically call the promises to manifest as they are already mine.

"Thank you, Lord, that as You diligently obeyed the voice of Your Father, to observe carefully all His commandments, in You I am set high above the nations of the earth. And all these blessings have come upon me and overtake me because You, Lord, obeyed the voice of the Father. I am blessed in the city and blessed in the country. My children are blessed, the work of my hands and the productivity of my business. I am blessed in the produce in my pantry and the food I prepare for my family. I am blessed when I come in and I am blessed when I go out. The Lord will continue to cause my enemies who rise up against me to be defeated before my face; they will come out against me one way and flee from me seven ways. The Lord has commanded a blessing in my bank accounts and in all to which I set my hand to, and He has blessed me in the land which the Lord my God has given me. And the Lord has granted me increase in my property, in my businesses and in all the activities of my family, in the land which the Lord has blessed me through the covenant that He cut for me through Jesus. The Lord has opened to me His good treasure, the heavens to give rain in my land in its season and has blessed all the work of my hand. I shall lend to many, but I shall not borrow. And the Lord has made me the head and not the tail, I am above and not beneath. In Him I will not turn aside from any of the words which He has commanded over me, and I confirm, that His covenant cut for me is my only declaration, spurning every idolatry that would try and corrupt my love for the Lord. Thank you for this indescribable gift, Jesus. Amen."

You can pick and choose those items that apply to your circumstances and leave out those that do not apply. I have prayed this scripture many times over my nation, declaring a blessing over it and over all the people in it. It is very powerful. Remember that the tense of our declaration, is present passive. Jesus HAS met all the conditions in this scripture for us; our part is to believe and to declare.

You may object to the way that I have prayed this scripture as in your mind, it is not factual. You may not have abundance now, and you may have been under oppression, and you currently do not flourish and thrive. Prayer is a matter of faith. We were translated from the kingdom of darkness to the kingdom of light by the confession of our mouths out of a heart that believed. Similarly, we declare the covenant promises that are ours in Christ and create with our words the very circumstances we desire. When I have sickness symptoms in my body, I do not confirm them, but declare that "by His stripes, I am healed". Am I lying? No. I am declaring the truth, and it will trump the apparent facts if I believe them. We do the same with the prayer out of Deuteronomy 28.

2 Cor 4:18 *while we do not look at the things which are seen, but at the things which are not seen. For the things which are seen are temporary, but the things which are not seen are eternal.*

You may see and feel the sickness in your body. But this is temporary. It will come to pass. As Christians we are instructed not to confirm these negative things which we can see and feel, but to call out the unseen promises which are yet to materialise. These things are eternal and will never pass away. So **aiteo** the promises of God and believe that you have them spiritually, and they will materialise. You are positionally healed in Christ. The natural will come in line with what you believe and what you **aiteo**.

Similarly, we can **aiteo** the promises in Malachi. Unfortunately, many preachers put condemnation on their congregants by the way that they apply Malachi chapter 3. They preach that we have to tithe or else we are under a curse as we have robbed God. No, and again

NO! Jesus was cursed for us on the tree, and even if we do not give or pay a tithe, we will never be under a curse. We know from Paul's writings that, as Christians, we should be the most generous of people and give abundantly because we have been blessed, and we cannot be cursed ever again.

I especially chose this scripture to give an example of praying an Old Testament promise as it is so widely misused. Again, I will personalise the promises in Mal 3:10-12 and leave out the negative parts:

"Lord, You have blessed me so abundantly that I have plenty to be able to give generously into my local church, and to all in need whom you direct me to bless. You have opened the windows of heaven and have poured out and continue to pour out a blessing over me that I do not have room enough to receive. You have rebuked the devourer for my sake, and he will not destroy the productivity of my labour. All peoples call me blessed for I live in a delightful land, and I have declared this according to the New Covenant in Your blood. Amen."

As a young Christian, I remember being confused by the word 'righteous', especially in Psalms. I read that the blessings and favour of God were for the righteous. I thought that these passages could not possibly apply to me as I was a sinner and certainly not holy or righteous. I needed a teacher to explain the proper meaning of righteousness as pertains to a Christian.

2 Cor 5:21 *For He* (God) *made Him* (Jesus) *who knew no sin to be sin for us, so that we might become the righteousness of God in Him.*

We cannot be righteous in and of ourselves. Good and moral behaviour will never make us righteous in God's sight. It took the death and resurrection of Jesus to deal with our sins, and now God views us as being righteous after we are born again. We are in Christ, and we are righteous as He is righteous. This is another example of the need for us to read Old Testament scriptures through the filter of our New Covenant rights. The promises for the righteous in Psalms and elsewhere are ours, because we are in Him.

In understanding the covenants, you can now be confident to take any promise in the Old Testament and declare it as yours and loose the blessings into your life.

New Covenant

Before we look at praying the Word out of the New Testament, let me ask you a question - the four accounts of the gospel, are they New Testament or Old Testament books? The compilers of our Bibles have put the divider of the change in the covenants between Malachi and Matthew. Many of us will answer this question as, "Of course the four accounts of the gospel are in the New Testament". However, most of what is said in the gospel accounts happen before the cross, so they were spoken under the Old Covenant. Therefore, as New Covenant believers, we must apply the Old Covenant promises carefully to ourselves to avoid the curses, and convert the future nature of the promises to, "He has already done it".

Quite a lot of what Jesus said was to raise the bar on the Law preached by the Pharisees, Sadducees and scribes. They had made the commandments of God of no effect by their traditions (Matt 15:6). So, we must be careful when we read the gospel accounts that we do not assume that everything Jesus said applies to us.

The Lord's Prayer

A good example of this is the Lord's Prayer. It is probably the best known and one of the most frequently spoken prayers in the world, and most people do not modify it to correctly apply it to us now. Most of the prayer is perfectly applicable to our lives as the matters prayed have 'passed through the cross' and are as applicable after the cross as they were before. Let us go through the prayer verse by verse.

Matt 6:9-10 *Our Father in heaven, hallowed* be Your *name. Your kingdom come. Your will be done on earth as it is in heaven.*

These two verses are praise to our God, and it is still our prayer that His will be done on the earth. No modification needed here as praise came through the cross and we are still expecting the kingdom to manifest on earth.

Matt 6:11 *Give us this day our daily bread.*

God will not provide our food by dispatching manna or quail for us to pick up as He did for the Israelites in the wilderness. Obviously, we know that, but I think we can expand this part of the prayer and make it more applicable to our personal needs. If we lack money for food, we can say, "Thank you, Lord, that I am more valuable than the birds of the air and so, you will provide for me so that I will eat today, as I seek first the Kingdom of God and Your righteousness" (Matt 6:26,33). If natural food is not an issue, we can say, "Bread of life, Jesus, I ask for the specific word I need today to strengthen me for the challenges that You know I will be facing today". Or "Healing is the children's bread, and as a child of the King, I **aiteo** for healing for my body today" (Matt 15:26).

Matt 6:12 *And forgive us our debts, as we forgive our debtors.*

We can read this verse to mean that if we do not forgive transgressions against us, God will not forgive us. This cannot be a prayer that we can pray straight up today, as we know that Jesus has paid for all our sins and transgressions on the cross - past, present and future. Therefore, we are forgiven. We can pray this verse like this: "I am forgiven of all my sins by the blood of Jesus, and so I am able, and empowered by the Holy Spirit, to forgive all those that have hurt me". If applicable, we can use this part of the prayer to confess a sin to the Father that comes to mind, knowing that we are already forgiven (1 John 1:9).

Matt 6:13a *And do not lead us into temptation, but deliver us from the evil one.*

In James 1:13 we are told that God cannot be tempted by evil, nor does He tempt anyone. The word 'tempt' and 'temptation' in Matthew and James are the same Greek word 'piradzo'. So, we cannot pray for the Lord not to lead us into temptation, as according to James, God does not deal with His people that way anymore. Also, according to James 4:7, God has instructed us to rebuke the devil. At the cross, the devil was defeated, and it is up to us to rebuke the devil and enforce Jesus' victory. So, we could pray instead, "Lord, You have given me the Word and the Holy Spirit so I can resist temptation, and as I am submitted to You, I rebuke the devil and he has to flee from me".

Matt 6:13b *For Yours is the kingdom and the power and the glory forever. Amen.*

Back to praise, and this part needs no modification, and we can pray it as it is written.

So remember, with the words, promises and prayers in the gospel accounts, we must know who is speaking, to whom and what is the context, before we apply them to our lives. The short question to ask is, "Is this before or after the cross?"

Moving into the rest of the New Testament, we find excellent prayers that we can pray as they are written, without need of any filter or modification. There is a treasure trove of prayers in the epistles (see the chapter on Paul's Prayers), and we should regularly use them in prayer as they provide us with a rich resource to pray both as kings and priests.

If it is Your Will

Most of us will be familiar with these words that Jesus prayed in the garden of Gethsemane. He was in agony as He prayed about what He was about to face on the cross.

Luke 22:42 *Father, if it is Your will, take this cup away from Me; nevertheless not My will but Yours, be done.*

Jesus prayed this very specific prayer in a unique situation. As He continued to pray, *His sweat became like great drops of blood falling down to the ground.* The mental trauma of knowing what He was about to face in the coming hours, was so horrific that He sweated blood. His prayer to the Father was very specific - is there another way to fulfil Your will? As we know, the way of the cross was the only way. Some Christians, in ignorance, use Jesus' words *if it be Your will* in their prayers because they are unsure what the will of God is in their situation. Hopefully, you have already gathered from this book, that the will of God has already been revealed to us in the Word, and we can be confident in prayer for matters that Jesus has already paid for on the cross. Praying "if it be Your will" for healing is a prayer of unbelief. It is an **erotao** type of prayer which cannot be answered as it is not prayed in faith.

There is a place for us to pray "if it be Your will". It is where the will of the Lord is not known.

James 4:13-15 *Come now, you who say, "Today or tomorrow we will go to such and such a city, spend a year there, buy and sell, and make a profit"; whereas you do not know what will happen tomorrow ... Instead, you ought to say, "If the Lord wills, we shall live and do this or that."*

1 Cor 4:19a *But I will come to you shortly, if the Lord wills.*

The will of God is clear in matters that are in the redemption plan of God. In Christ we have healing, peace, deliverance and salvation etc, and these are freely available for us to appropriate through faith. But we need to seek the Lord for His plan for our lives when it comes to matters that are unique to ourselves - which city we will live in, and the business we should conduct, and the plethora of decisions we need to make for our personal lives. We should pray "if it is Your will", as we seek the Lord's wisdom and guidance for our daily lives. In these circumstances, we will be praying in faith that the Lord will guide us to make the right decisions. But where the will of God is known, we cannot pray "if it be Your will".

DANIEL'S PRAYERS

An important aspect of prayer is timing. We know from Mark 11:23-24 that we receive the answer when we pray. The Lord has heard our prayer and positionally, we have the answer. But there is often a delay before the manifestation of the answer and, as we do not understand why there is a delay, we often make excuses for the delay or even change our theology to match the circumstances. If we pray according to the principles of prayer that we have already studied in this book, then what is the explanation for the delay? The delay in the answer to Daniel's prayer, which was demonic interference, is often cited as a possible reason for the delay in the answer to our own prayers. So let us look at Daniel's prayers, and hopefully 'put to bed' this excuse.

In Daniel chapters 9 and 10, we see Daniel praying twice, and he experienced different time periods in which he received the answers.

Dan 9:21-22a *yes, while I was speaking in prayer, the man Gabriel ... reached me about the time of the evening offering. And he informed me and talked with me.*

Here Daniel received the answer to his prayer immediately.

Dan 10:2 *In those days I, Daniel, was mourning three full weeks.*

Dan 10:10-13 *Suddenly, a hand touched me ... And he (the angel) said to me ... for from the first day that you set your heart to understand, and to humble yourself before your God, your words were heard; and I have come because of your words. But the prince of the kingdom of Persia withstood me twenty-one days; and behold, Michael, one of the chief princes came to help me, for I had been left alone there with the kings of Persia.*

The second time Daniel prayed, it took three weeks for him to receive the answer to his prayer. Gabriel told him why. A demonic principality resisted Gabriel and fought with him to prevent the message getting through to Daniel. I surmise that the first time he prayed, the devil was caught off guard, not paying attention to what Daniel was doing at that time, and Gabriel could get through to Daniel immediately as there was no opposition. The second time, the prince of Persia, a demonic principality, was watching Daniel, and when he realised that this was a prayer of import, he was ready to resist the answer getting through. That must have been a massive battle, for Michael had to be called in to overcome the prince of Persia.

This account leads to a question: "Do we suffer delays to our prayers today in the same way?" Remember that Daniel was living in a time before the cross and the devil was still the ruler of the earth. His principality, the prince of Persia, had full authority to resist Gabriel, and it came down to who was stronger of the two. When Michael joined the fight, the two archangels could overcome the prince of Persia, and Gabriel could complete his mission.

We read in Rev 12:11 *And they overcame him* (the accuser of the brethren, the devil) *by the blood of the Lamb and the word of their testimony.* Because of Jesus taking the keys of hell and the grave from the devil, he has no more authority to resist the Word or the work of angels. So, like Daniel with his first prayer, we can be confident that God has answered our prayer immediately. That does not mean that the manifestation of the subject of our prayer is immediate. There can be many reasons for delays. For example, a mother may immediately answer the request of her son positively but there is a condition on the timing of the manifestation. The son asks, "Mom, I am hungry. Please can I eat?" The mom answers, "Certainly. But you will have to wait for supper time as I am still cooking". The son has had his answer, but the manifestation is delayed. Assuming we have prayed correctly and have avoided the error spoken of in James 4:1-3, we can be confident of a positive answer from the Lord.

2 Cor 1:20 *For all the promises of God in Him are Yes, and in Him Amen, to the glory of God through us.*

Notice the condition in this scripture - in Him. If we are in Him and He in us, then our requests are according to His will and our prayers are **aiteo** in nature. We have the promises positionally, and we can wait for the manifestation with eager anticipation; supper time is coming. We just need a bit of patience.

Heb 6:12b *those who through faith and patience inherit the promises.*

When our prayer is not an **aiteo**, but an **erotao** for something that we are not certain is God's will, and the situation we are praying about involves other people, we will usually face delays in the manifestation. If we are praying to be blessed with a job, a spouse or an opportunity, there are other people that need to hear God and fall in line with the plan He has for us and the other person. This may take time for it to happen, and we need to be patient for the manifestation of the answer to our prayer.

Aiteo prayer is straight forward as we know the will of God in the matter. But when we are praying for direction, or wisdom to decide between several options, the path to the answer to our prayer is a bit more complicated. We need the help of the Holy Spirit to make known to us the will of God in a particular situation we are praying about. We need His peace to be our umpire and for Him to highlight the Word that shines light in our situation.

Col 3:15-16a *And let the peace of God rule in your hearts, to which you were called in one body; and be thankful. Let the word of Christ dwell in you richly in all wisdom.*

The Holy Spirit will, by peace and quickening to us the scriptures, show us which option is the best answer to our prayer. I do not say this is easy, and does require us to press into God, seeking Him diligently. Also, notice in the above scripture, that Paul says that *you were called in one body*. The body of Christ, the Church, can be a great source of strength and wisdom for us, and we can seek guidance from the elders and leaders of the community that we are part of. We do not have to do it alone.

Quick fixes are not usually God's answer to our prayer, and we should be prepared to be patient for God's solution to manifest. We do not want to be like Abram who ran out of patience, listened to his wife, and made another plan. The result was Ishmael, which was not God's plan at all. Let us be patient and stay in faith as our answer is on the way. How many people have lost faith and patience and have given up before seeing the manifestation? They undo their prayer by saying things like, "I do not think that God wants me to have it afterall", or "It seems that I do not deserve God's blessing in this way". The angel, who was just about to knock on the door with the answer, would be sent away by the negative words of doubt and unbelief. Abraham had to wait for 25 years for Isaac. God came through when the time was right. We do not have 20:20 vision of what is happening around us in the spirit, and especially into the future. Only God knows the perfect answer to our prayer, so stay the course and never, never give up.

I am sure you have heard the saying 'the heavens are like brass', and 'my prayers do not go higher than the ceiling', and 'we do not have an open heaven so our prayers cannot get through'. These are excuses as to why we are not getting answers to our prayers and mostly they are uttered out of desperation, emotion or unbelief. Let us not let the circumstances and the way we feel take us off the Word or the direction that the Holy Spirit has shown us by His peace. It is good for us to remember the often quoted saying - 'Never doubt in the dark what God told you in the light'. We should stay plugged into God and not be moved by circumstances, fear or doubt.

There is another fallacy that can get us into bondage. Some say that there are certain places on the earth that are best for prayer as there is a portal direct into heaven from there. I do not find this in the Bible, and we must avoid such new-age mumbo jumbo. The occult and certain false religions have special places in which they pray and have ceremonies. I do not doubt that this gets them into the spirit, but which spirit? Certainly not the Spirit of God. As prayer is by faith, we can pray anywhere at any time and the Lord hears us.

Eph 6:13b-14a *and having done all, to stand. Stand therefore.*

When you have done all that you know to do ... stand. Do not give up ... stand. Do not make another plan ... stand. God's way is always the best. Stay in faith and have patience to receive His promise. It will come.

PRAYING FOR THE LOST

Praying for a loved one, relative or friend can be one of the most difficult things to do consistently and on a protracted basis. How easy it would be if we could pray kingly prayer over the person and demand that they receive Christ. But even the Lord will not violate our free will, and so we can only pray priestly prayers for them.

Any of Paul's prayers that seem appropriate to you can be prayed over people to repent and come to Christ. There is a very powerful scripture that we can pray for the lost.

2 Cor 4:3-4,6 *But even if our gospel is veiled, it is veiled to those who are perishing, whose minds the god of this age has blinded, who do not believe, lest the light of the gospel of the glory of Christ, who is the image of God, should shine on them. For it is the God who commanded light to shine out of darkness, who has shone in our hearts to give the light of the knowledge of the glory of God in the face of Jesus Christ.*

The god of this age, the devil, has blinded the eyes of those who do not believe in Jesus. The devil will use religion, evolution, science, past hurts and lies and deception to prevent unbelievers from seeing the light of the gospel. We can break through this blindness by asking for God to command the light of the knowledge of Jesus to shine in their situation - for a Christian to speak the life of Jesus to the person, for an encounter with God in some event, in a book or movie etc.

Most of the time, we do not know how we should pray for people, especially for those that are not born again, and after we have exhausted our words, we can pray in tongues. We will discuss this in the next chapter and suffice it for now to look at an intriguing scripture in Romans in this regard.

Rom 8:26-27 *Likewise the Spirit also helps our weakness. For we do not know what we should pray for as we ought, but the Spirit Himself makes intercession for us with groanings which cannot be uttered. Now He who searches the hearts knows what the mind of the Spirit is, because He makes intercession for the saints according to the will of God.*

I cut my intercession teeth on this scripture, and I studied each word to try and understand the significance of what Paul was saying here. We will expand on this scripture in the next chapter, and for now all I want to say is that it is very powerful when we pray for others in the Spirit as He helps us in our weakness. That weakness is not knowing how to pray correctly in the situation or for the person, but He helps us. He does not take over. The word 'help' in the Greek means 'together with against'. He helps us overcome when we do not know how to pray, but we still have to do the praying. How awesome is the providence of our God who always makes a way for us to succeed!

INTERCESSION

In the 1980s and 90s intercession was a real buzz word and I aspired to qualify to the dizzy heights of being known as an intercessor. The big-name preachers all had their intercessory teams and often there was one person, usually a woman, who was known as Preacher X's intercessor. Wow!

Eventually I got over this awe and realised that we are all called to intercession, and it is not a title, it is a function.

1 Tim 2:1 *Therefore I exhort first of all that supplications, prayers, intercessions, and giving of thanks be made for all men.*

In Eph 6:18 Paul says to pray *with all perseverance and supplications for all the saints.*

The context of many references to intercession is to prevent calamity upon those who are not God's people - Gen 18:16 where Abraham intercedes for Sodom and Gomorrah; Ezek 22:30 where God seeks for a man to stand in the gap; Matt 9:38 where we are instructed to pray for the Lord to send labourers into the harvest. In these instances, the subject of the intercession is the unsaved. However, Christians also get into trouble and need the intervention of God in their lives. Jesus is constantly interceding for us (Heb 7:25 and Rom 8:34) and likewise, we are to intercede for those in need, whether saved or unsaved.

Rom 8:26 *Likewise the Spirit also helps in our weaknesses. For we do not know what we should pray for as we ought, but the Spirit Himself makes intercession for us with groanings which cannot be uttered.*

This deep intercession prayed from the depths of our spirit, like the groanings of a woman giving birth, leads us to understand that this type of prayer is for the unsaved to be born again into Christ.

Furthermore, Paul is describing intercession for the saints in Gal 4:19 *My little children, for whom I labour in birth again until Christ is formed in you.* It seems that he interceded for them to be born again and then again for them to mature in Christ. This intercession is deep travail, 'labour in birth', where it is the Holy Spirit praying through us, in groanings that we cannot articulate in words.

Groanings in Rom 8:26 can be scary for us to contemplate as it sounds so strange and super-spiritual. If we realise that the Spirit of God abides in our spirit and *out of our heart will flow rivers of living water* (John 7:38), then we should trust the Lord that this process of travail is the spiritual version of a baby being born in the natural. Many great men have written extensively on this subject. (I recommend John Alcock's book - How to pray with God. It is an excellent practical guide to intercession.) So, I just want to introduce the subject as part of our priestly prayer ministry.

It is very interesting in Rom 8:26-27, where intercession is mentioned twice, that there are two slightly different words used for intercession.

In Rom 8:26 *the Spirit Himself makes intercession for us*, the word intercession is huperentunchano - on behalf of someone, to entreat. In the NKJV, the translators included 'for us' in the sentence whereas other versions leave this out. The NKJV included 'for us' to try and translate the 'huper' before 'entunchano' to signify that the Spirit is interceding on our behalf. In verse 27 *He makes intercession for the saints according to the will of God*, the word intercession is 'entunchano' without the 'huper'. So, we could expand these two verses as follows which brings more clarity to the agency of the Holy Spirit in our prayer:

Rom 8:26-27 from a position in us, the Holy Spirit does the praying through us, on our behalf, as in our weakness, we do not know how to pray as we should. He (and in context, this is Jesus) takes the prayer that the Holy Spirit is praying through us, knowing exactly what the mind of the Holy Spirit in this request is, and He presents it perfectly to the Father (my paraphrase).

So, praying in the Spirit is the most effective way to pray our priestly prayer for others as it is direct from the Holy Spirit to Jesus to the Father. We are the conduit, and our understanding does not get in the way. What a wonderful provision the Lord has made for us to overcome our limitations as mortal men and women.

Standing in the Gap

In my early days as a Christian, I attended many prayer meetings where we prayed for people, standing in the gap for them as described in Job 1:10. Their fence was down, and they were being attacked by the devil. We stood in the gap in their hedge and fought off the devil for them. I cannot remember exactly how we prayed, but I know that my imagination was fired up fighting the devil and his hordes off the person we were praying for. Many years later, I concede that there is some truth in the way we were praying, but for the most part, we were beating the air with our words, hoping to make a difference.

The principle probably originates from a combination of three scriptures:

Job 1:9-12 *So Satan answered the Lord and said, "Does Job fear God for nothing? Have You not made a hedge around him, around his household, and around all that he has on every side?" ... And the Lord said to Satan, "Behold all that he has is in your power; only do not lay a hand on his person."*

Ezek 22:30 *So I sought for a man among them who would make a wall, and stand in the gap before Me on behalf of this land, that I should not destroy it; but I found no one.*

Is 59:16 *He saw that there was no man, and wondered that there was no intercessor.*

The problem is that apart from a word of knowledge, we cannot know enough about the person's circumstances to know where the gap in their hedge is, and how we are to plug their defences. Really, it is only Jesus who can stand in the gap, as in Job 9:33 *Nor is there any mediator between us, who may lay his hand on us both.* He permanently plugged the gap in our hedge made by sin with His sacrifice on the cross and that is why He is continually interceding for us.

In Job 1:12 it is believed that Job was in Satan's hands because he was operating in fear, which opened the hedge for the devil to attack him. Also, it is thought that Job was not in covenant with God, as he was not a descendant of Abraham, and therefore was vulnerable to Satan's attack. These questions are only of academic interest and what is important for us to know is that Satan now has no access to a New Covenant believer's life if access is not given to him by agreeing to his lies. We have a covenant with God bought by the blood of Jesus which enables us to resist the attack of the devil.

We can avoid phony spiritual warfare against the devil by sticking to the Word and doing our part in priestly prayer and interceding for people.

TONGUES

1 Cor 14:14-15 *For if I pray in a tongue, my spirit prays, but my understanding is unfruitful. What is the conclusion then? I will pray with the spirit, and I will also pray with the understanding. I will sing with the spirit, and I will also sing with the understanding.*

I am sure you have had the experience of running out of words when praying. We do not want to get into 'vain repetitions', so I am grateful to the Lord for providing us with another way we can pray when we do not know how to pray any further. Paul's prayers give us many more scriptures that we can pray, but even these will run out eventually and that is when we can pray in tongues. We have seen in the previous chapter how, in our weakness and not knowing how to pray, we can rely on the Holy Spirit to pray through us which Rom 8:26 calls *groanings which cannot be uttered*. Some translations say that it is groanings that we cannot utter in articulate speech. The heart of God for that situation can get so intense it comes out like the groanings of a travailing woman.

Jude 1:20-21 *But you, beloved, building yourselves up on your most holy faith, praying in the Holy Spirit, keeping yourself in the love of God, looking for the mercy of our Lord Jesus Christ unto eternal life.*

Praying in tongues, as the Spirit gives you utterance, is very powerful as it not only builds up your faith for the matter you are praying about, but it enables you to pray into very difficult situations where you need to stay in the love and mercy of God in order to be able to even pray. Jesus instructs us in Matt 5:44 *love your enemies, bless those who curse you, do good to those who hate you, and pray for those that spitefully use you and persecute you.* There is no way we have the ability to do this without God's help. Usually we do not want to even see a person who has hurt us, never mind bless them and do good to them. However, we can if we do it God's way. We do not know how to pray for them and to bless them, but we can pray in the Spirit and release the love and mercy of God towards the person. We might still feel wounded by that person, but God still loves them, and He wants us to release them His way. The result of our prayer is that we have built ourselves up in our most holy faith and we can walk in freedom that is only possible in Him.

In 1 Cor 14:18 Paul said that he spoke in tongues more than them all. We have seen in an earlier chapter how often in the epistles Paul records his prayers for the churches. But even he would have eventually run out of words to pray, and his concern for the people would have motivated him to continue to pray for them in tongues. Praying in tongues is a very powerful priestly prayer, and we can pray this way always in all circumstances as it does not engage our minds; the Holy Spirit is praying through us, and we can be driving a car or working a job at the same time. Praying in tongues is the only way we can obey the instruction in 1 Thess 5:17 to *pray without ceasing.*

I believe that we are mainly praying priestly prayers when we pray in the Spirit. However, sometimes I have found myself praying, and very forceful tongues come out of my mouth. It seems like kingly prayer as it comes out as demanding or rebuking. Sometimes we simply do not understand what we are doing and, if we are in control and can stop it any time, then go with the flow. We should not limit God, and we certainly do not understand everything in the scriptures. So, trust God in this way to pray despite not understanding all that is going on. Praying in the Spirit is such a powerful way to pray, that we certainly need it in our prayer toolbox.

SPIRITUAL WARFARE

In a book on prayer, we cannot avoid this topic. In my early Christian walk, there were sometimes prayer meetings held in high places of the city. On a hill overlooking the town or city, or in a tall building, we rebuked the devil as we prayed for the city. I was involved in this a few times as I was growing up in the Lord, but I did not really understand it. It was certainly exciting, but I was dubious, even then, as to how effective it was. We bound the evil spirits harassing the city and loosed the angels to bring blessing to the people.

Let us look at this scripturally, as the purpose of this book is to become more effective in prayer. We do not want to *run uncertainly; not as one who beats the air* as Paul says in 1 Cor 9:26.

2 Cor 10:3-4 *For though we walk in the flesh, we do not war according to the flesh. For the weapons of our warfare are not carnal but mighty in God for pulling down strongholds, casting down arguments and every high thing that exalts itself against the knowledge of God, bringing every thought into captivity to the obedience of Christ.*

You can see that our warfare is not seen but is in the realm of words and thoughts. Therefore, we engage spiritual warfare in our souls and minds. Jesus defeated the devil on the cross through His perfect sacrifice, and the only weapon the devil has now is deception. He will attack us in our thoughts, like he did with Eve, and question our faith and the Word of God and try to bring us under condemnation. This is the arena of our warfare, and we have to be diligent, as the scripture says, to control our thoughts and keep them in line with the Word. Jesus defeated the devil in the wilderness by quoting the scripture appropriate to the lie that the devil attacked Him with. We are to do the same. We change our circumstances with our words; we **aiteo** because we know our covenant rights.

James 4:7 *Therefore submit to God. Resist the devil and he will flee from you.*

We submit to God's Word and renew our minds to its truth. Then we can speak the Word and, just like Jesus experienced in the wilderness, the devil flees, and we have won that battle. A great man of God once said, "You cannot keep a bird from flying over your head, but you sure can keep him from landing on your head and building a nest." Thoughts will come and attack your mind, but we are to rebuke them and give them no space to stay. One wrong thought builds its nest in our head and can leaven or corrupt our whole outlook on life and the way we conduct ourselves.

Paul, in Ephesians chapter 6, gives us the most comprehensive instruction on how to war in the spirit, both defensively and offensively.

Eph 6:10-18 *Finally, my brethren, be strong in the Lord and in the power of His might. Put on the whole armour of God, that you may be able to stand against the wiles of the devil. For we do not wrestle against flesh and blood, against the rulers of the darkness of this age, against spiritual hosts of wickedness in the heavenly places. Therefore take up the whole armour of God, that you may be able to withstand in the evil day, and having done all, to stand. Stand therefore, having girded your waist with truth, having put on the breastplate of righteousness, and having shod your feet with the preparation of the gospel of peace; above all, taking the shield of faith with which you will be able to quench all the fiery darts of the wicked one. And take the helmet of salvation and the sword of the Spirit, which is the word of God; praying always with all prayer and supplication in the Spirit, being watchful to this end with all perseverance and supplication for all saints.*

There is a lot that we could unpack from this scripture, and there is excellent teaching on the armour of God. For this chapter I just want to highlight the main points pertaining to warring correctly in the spirit in the context of prayer.

Any soldier knows that he has defensive armour and offensive weapons. Both are very important if he is to survive the battle. The defensive armour in this scripture is the girdle, the breastplate, the sandals, the shield and the helmet. The offensive weapon is the sword. Paul has given us the natural metaphor of a Roman soldier's armour so we can understand the spiritual truth that he wishes to convey.

We are to gird our waist with truth like a belt. The soldier's belt was broad and heavy and supported and protected his midriff. There was a protective piece hanging down from the front of it and the belt carried his sword. As the belt provided strength for the soldier's core and protected his loins, so does the truth of the Word protect and strengthen the soldier of Christ against the lies of the devil. The sword of the Word is always found in truth, and ready for use whenever required to defeat the enemy.

In the Word, righteousness speaks of pure clothing which we are given when we are born again. Our filthy rags of sin are removed, and we are clothed in God's pure garments of righteousness. The evidence that we are made right with God is worn as a breastplate which protects our heart. The devil tries to attack our heart with lies, saying that we are not worthy because of some sin we have committed. It is so important that we defeat the lie with the truth which says that we are made righteous by the blood of Jesus, not by our attempts to be righteous ourselves. Prov 4:23 *Keep your heart with all diligence, for out of it spring the issues of life.* We cannot resist the devil if we are defeated in our heart.

A soldier's feet are extremely important. If they are hurt, he cannot march and keep up with the army. Note the scripture says we must put on our feet the preparation of the gospel of peace. The road we walk can be made rough and difficult by the fears that the devil tries to sow into our mind. However, knowing *the peace of God, which surpasses all understanding, will guard your hearts and minds through Christ Jesus* (Phil 4:7). The good news of who we are in Christ, gives us peace and enables us to overcome and fight on.

Faith quenches the fiery arrows of the devil. He will bombard us with doubts and lies trying to get through to us and wound us. Faith is our response to God's grace. If we know what God has provided for us in the New Covenant, we can use the Word to protect us from the lies of the devil. Jesus, in the temptation in the wilderness, knew the Word so well that he could deflect the devil's attempts to twist the Word and use it inappropriately to defeat Him in his mission. Jesus knew how to use the shield of faith and with it He quenched the devil's fiery darts.

A soldier's helmet protects his head, and without protection, a blow can totally immobilize him and even kill him. The Greek word in this scripture for salvation is 'soteria' meaning deliverance from peril, danger and destruction. Accepting Jesus' sacrifice for us on the cross saves us from destruction in this life and in the one to come, and so it is essential that we are protected by God's provision of salvation to defeat the devil. It's interesting that to be saved we believe in our heart that Jesus is Lord, and we confess with our mouths that Jesus rose from the dead (Rom10:9). When we are born again, salvation protects our thoughts and we know that we are sons of God, victorious soldiers in His army.

The sword of the Spirit is the only offensive weapon in this scripture. After ensuring that every part of our being is protected by the Word, we can aggress towards the enemy and apply the Word of God in any situation, under the guidance of the Spirit, to bring about deliverance. Firstly, we need to know our covenant rights to **aiteo** the word and bring deliverance for ourselves, but also the main use of the sword is in verse 18. We are to pray with the sword with all kinds of prayer and supplication for all saints. This is the crux of this passage of scripture. All the pieces of armour in this scripture are important and they enable us protect ourselves from the devil. But that is not the end of it. The purpose of the whole passage is to show us that we need to protect ourselves so that we are strong enough to wield the sword of the Spirit in prayer for others. This is our fight of faith.

The real spiritual battle is within, in our thoughts and words. Yes, there is definitely a war going on in the spirit. Elisha showed his servant the reality of the spiritual battle going on around them in 2 Kings 6:16-17. The Lord opened the eyes of Elisha's servant, and he saw that the mountain was full of horses and chariots of fire all around. Also, in Dan 10:13, Gabriel told Daniel that the prince of the kingdom of Persia resisted him 21 days, and the archangel Michael had to help him overcome and get the message from God through to Daniel. There are many other examples from the scriptures and so we know that the angels of God are constantly warring with the devil and his demons to bring us the answers to our prayers. But nowhere in the scriptures do we see the saints of God physically warring in the spiritual realm as, unlike the angels, we are clothed in flesh. Yes, people have seen angels, demons and even the devil, but we are never instructed to war in that realm ourselves. Some have been physically assaulted by demons and often rendered paralysed in the encounter. They had no strength 'to war' against the demon. But we can war with our words and that is usually how these demonic attacks are ended - by calling on the name of the Lord and declaring our position as sons of God. We submit to God, resist the devil with our words, and he has to flee. Battle won.

When we want to pray for our city, our nation or our community, remember that we can only affect demonic influence with our words. The devil can operate in a place because he has been given permission to do so by the sins of the people who live there. We will have limited effect by praying the Word over a whole city in a general way, unless by revelation from the Holy Spirit to do this (and I definitely do not want to limit our praying this way if the Lord instructs us to do so). What is certain, and scriptural, is to pray for the people specifically, that the light of the glorious gospel of Christ would shine on and in the lost, that they may repent and turn from their wicked ways. When the people turn away from evil, and embrace Jesus, then the devil cannot stay. In the 1800s in the USA, Brother Nash went ahead of Charles Finney a few weeks before his revival meetings and prayed. He did not fight the evil spirits operating in those towns; he prayed for the people to see Jesus. Then the gospel was preached by Finney, and whole towns and cities turned from sin and were saved. So let us be purposeful in our prayers, and we will be very effective if we stay scriptural. Then we will see things change.

KING OF KINGS, LORD OF LORDS AND THE HIGH PRIEST OF OUR CONFESSION

As we come to the end of our study on praying as kings and priests, I want to conclude by bringing us back to the beginning. Why are there so many scriptures in the Bible encouraging us to pray, with instruction and with examples? Surely prayer should be a priority in our lives, and unless we know what we are doing and why we are doing it, we will not fulfil our mandate to *pray without ceasing* (1 Thess 5:17).

I find the scripture in 1 Tim 6:11-16 a marvellous summary of the instructions from our Lord: *But you, O man of God, flee these things* (in the verse before, Paul is warning Timothy about the love of money) *and pursue righteousness, godliness, faith, love, patience, gentleness. Fight the good fight of faith, lay hold of eternal life, to which you were also called and have confessed the good confession in the presence of many witnesses. I urge you in the sight of God who gives life to all things, and before Christ Jesus who witnessed the good confession before Pontius Pilate, that you keep this commandment without spot, blameless until our Lord Jesus Christ's appearing, which He will manifest in His own time, He who is the blessed and only Potentate, the King of kings and Lord of lords, who alone has immortality, dwelling in unapproachable light, whom no man has seen or can see, to whom be honour and everlasting power. Amen.*

We are called both to rule on this earth as kings under King Jesus bringing heaven to earth, and to operate as priests under Lord Jesus, ambassadors ministering to the needs of the people of the earth.

Heb 3:1 *Therefore, holy brethren, partakers of the heavenly calling, consider the Apostle and High Priest of our confession, Christ Jesus.*

Christ Jesus is the source (apostle) and High Priest of our confession, and it is our heavenly calling to bring His people, both born again and not, in our priestly service to our High Priest who is seated at the right hand of the Father and is continually making intercession for us.

In the last book in the Bible, the Revelation of Jesus Christ, Jesus is introduced first in Rev 1:5-6 *Jesus Christ, the faithful witness, the firstborn from the dead, and the ruler over the kings of the earth. To Him who loved us and washed us from our sins in His own blood, and has made us kings and priests to His God and Father, to Him be glory and dominion forever and ever. Amen.*

What a magnificent partnership - kings and lords under the almighty King and Lord Jesus, and priests under our High Priest Jesus, seated in heavenly places. How astounding it is that God consulted with Abraham before He destroyed Sodom and Gomorrah. Gen 18:17 *And the Lord said, "Shall I hide from Abraham what I am doing?"* Abraham, God's covenant partner in the earth, consulted with His earthly partner and received the intercession from Abraham as he asked to spare the lives of the people in those cities, if some righteous people could be found there. What astonishing power this is for the Creator of the universe to ask a mere man his opinion on the matter. It could only happen because of covenant. As ambassadors and priests of our God, we have the same privilege as Abraham, which is also a great responsibility, as our covenant is far more powerful than Abraham's, because it is ratified in the blood of our Lord.

I have concentrated on expounding on the scriptures about prayer in this book, and very little on my testimonies of answered prayer and on my own prayer disciplines. I have done this as the scriptures are eternal, and my experiences in prayer are only of limited benefit to you, the reader. I wanted you to have the foundation in the Word, for you to be discipled by the Holy Spirit, as I was. Please do not think that this teaching is theory only. I have prayed countless hours, lead many prayer meetings and have seen the answers to many prayers offered up on my own, with my wife and family, and in public meetings. I have seen prayer answered supernaturally in my personal life, in my family and church and in my nation. Know that prayer works, and it works very effectively, if we take the principles expounded in this book and put them into practice. I would love to hear your stories of how this book has helped you to become effective in prayer. See my email address in the front of this book.

All that remains is for me to repeat Paul's instruction to Timothy:

1 Tim 6:13-14 *I urge you in the sight of God who gives life to all things, and before Christ Jesus ... that you keep this commandment* (fight the good fight of a good confession) *without spot, blameless until our Lord Jesus Christ's appearing.*

I trust you have enjoyed reading this book and have been challenged in your prayer life. I hope that you will take these principles and ... **PRAY!**

"Prayer is not learned in a classroom, but in the closet." (E M Bounds)